Covert Manipulation

How to Take Control of Personal Relationships, Influencing Human Behavior Through Emotional Intelligence and Body Language

Bran Deep

Table of Contents

Introduction

Salespeople are the same, their livelihood depends on persuading you to buy the products they are advertising. They are skilled at their craft and employ various psychological techniques in order to convince you to cave in and make a purchase. Think about car salesmen and how well-known they are for their selling abilities. You have to be pretty good to persuade someone to buy a used car. Pretty impressive, right?

Without a doubt, we can say that persuasion is a distinctly powerful tool, and these people are powerful for being in its possession. But why is that? And why are we so quick to flock to people who seem to have this gift of convincing, from individuals, to masses of people? The art of persuasion is of significant importance in our society, whether we realize it or not. Some of us are better at it than others, but we are all constantly trying to convince someone else of one thing or another. But what is it that actually makes a person more convincing? That is what we are going to find out.

The short answer is that there is no "one thing" that will make you convincing, but that it is a combined effect of several factors that come into play. In order to figure out what they are, you need to carefully study a person of great persuasive influence. What is their body language like? Do they have a certain facial expression? What tonality are they using?

You see, each and every one of things is vitally important when you are trying to persuade someone, even if, at first glance, they might not seem meaningful. People are extremely susceptible to subtle details like these, even if they are not aware of it. It has a lot to do with how these things affect us on a subconscious level, from a psychological point of view.

Studies have shown that we are more easily persuaded by a person who displays confidence. It makes sense, because when we see a person saying something with confidence, we automatically assume that they know what they are talking about, when in reality, they might be bluffing. Especially because humans are so often lacking in confidence, when someone else seems to have it, we naturally doubt ourselves and tend to be persuaded by this other person that we perceive as more confident in their knowledge and abilities.

Persuasion is, indeed, an art form, and one that not everyone can engage in. It takes a special kind of charisma, in order to be able to do it, and you have to pay attention to every little detail, from facial expressions, to tonality, to body language and choose your words very carefully. Convincing people is no easy task. However, fortunately for us, it is something that can be taught, learned and practiced. With a little bit of help and guidance, you will be able to persuade people in no time.

The first thing you have to learn is to build confidence in yourself. Remember, if you don't believe in yourself and what you are saying, neither will other people. Confidence can be gained and practiced. The secret is to surround yourself with positivity and to keep sending optimistic messages to yourself. Start every day with a positive thought about yourself and your abilities; keep reminding yourself how great you are.

Slowly, but surely, you will get used to this new state of mind that you acquire. You will start feeling more comfortable with yourself and with other people and you will no longer feel intimidated by others who display confidence. You will build up the courage to defend and argument your point of view with a fierceness and determination that you were lacking before and you will gradually become more and more authoritative and persuasive, just through your change in attitude.

Of course, this is merely the foundation upon which you have to continue to build, in order to truly become a persuasive person. From here on out, you need to work on everything: from verbal abilities, to body language, to energy, tonality and facial expressions. Each and every one of these things contributes in its own unique way to the overall impression that you leave on people. The way people perceive you; your confidence and your power of persuasion is heavily influenced by these details. Fortunately, these are things that you can work on, tweak, chisel and learn, in order to maximize the potential of your persuasion skills.

This is why, in the following chapters, we are going to insist on each one and go into detail about why they are so important, how you can use each persuasion tool in the right way, as well as plenty of tips and tricks that will help you improve in each particular area.

Chapter 1: What is Covert Manipulation?

Covert refers to the emotional manipulation that takes place being performed in a secretive, subtle or underhanded way. Think of covert manipulators as undercover agents on a mission to rob you of your sanity and happiness. The covert aspect of the emotional manipulation is one of the reasons it is so dangerous.

When we know something, or someone is bad for us we know to be careful and have our guard up. Our defenses are raised, and we are on the look out for harm and ways to protect ourselves from it. Covert manipulators take aware this foresight from us. They are wolves in sheep's clothing attempting to appear harmless and benign in order for us to drop our guard.

There is an old Chinese expression that translates roughly as 'Daggers are hidden in smiles'. This refers to the fact that often the most charming, friendly people, at least on the surface, will turn out to be the most dangerous and threatening. This is certainly the case with covert emotional manipulators.

Don't for one second think that an emotionally manipulative person will be obvious or easy to spot. Far from it. It is a cruel and bitter irony that often the people who appear to be the best for us turn out to be the worst. The person who seems like Prince Charming or The Perfect Girlfriend will often turn out to be the spouse or partner from hell. That best friend who seems to know exactly what to say to you and how and when to say it may well turn out to be the worst thing that ever happened to you. And that powerful ally at work who seems to be your teammate and partner on the road to success could well turn out to be a snake in the grass that sought your downfall all along.

Not all manipulation, or manipulators, are covert. Some people will be obviously trying to influence you or emotionally blackmail you. While these types of people can be harmful, they are far less dangerous than covert manipulators. Think of the difference between a poisonous snake that is brightly colored and stands out from its environment and one that is camouflaged and blends in. Both can be deadly. However, the brightly colored snake is one which you know to stay well away from. The camouflaged snake is likely to be overlooked until it is too late and its fangs are sunk into you. Consider the hidden snake to be the manipulator and this book to be your antidote.

Emotional

Now that we understand exactly what is meant by the 'covert' aspect of emotional manipulation, it is important to consider the emotional side. There are various types of manipulation of which emotional manipulation is but one.

Unlike other types of manipulation, such as physical or financial, emotional manipulation can be harder to spot. It is easy to recognize when someone is being physically abusive as we are likely to feel pain and recognize the situation as one which should not be taking place. Financial manipulation is clear too as it is obvious when someone is not trying to hide the fact they are seeking to financially leach from us. Emotional manipulation, however, is far more subtle and hard to detect.

It is sad but true that many people do not have a clear understanding of their own emotional landscape. We live in a culture and world in which emotional behavior and understanding is not often promoted or supported. If people are unaware of their own emotions and how they impact upon them it can be incredibly difficult to realize when someone is manipulating us emotionally. There are several reasons for this.

One reason why emotional manipulation is so hard to spot is because a skilled manipulator will be able to make the emotional experience of knowing them one which is not straightforward. If we were emotionally manipulated in a way which only felt bad all of the time, then it would be difficult for the emotional manipulation to continue for a prolonged period of time. The best emotional manipulators know this and so act in a way which makes the experience emotionally confusing for the person involved.

Emotional manipulation is like a drug. It can feel good at first but over the long term it is likely to destroy the life of the person who is a victim of it. Also like a drug addict, people who are being emotionally manipulated are likely to feel they have control of a situation long after the power has been taken out of their hands.

Think of a person's emotional makeup as like a language. A skilled emotional manipulator will take the time to learn the language of an individual in order to be able to speak directly to them in a way which no one else seems able to. The best manipulators are able to understand a person's motivations, desires and fears and use them to great effect. If each emotion a person experiences is like a string, controlling a different part of their life, then think of an emotional manipulator as the puppet master, pulling on the strings and controlling the person in the way that the manipulator desires.

Chapter 2: How to identify yourself as the Victim of Covert Manipulation

No one likes being manipulated. When manipulation occurs, you lose your power and your will. You must do what the other person wants. You often have no idea what the other person is really planning and you have no say in the situation. This makes life very difficult and it can cause you to do things that you don't want to do.

Now that you know the secrets to covert manipulation, you also know what to watch out for. You can reverse the techniques in this book to see when others are manipulating you. You can also flip these tactics on people and give them the manipulation that they are trying to run on you. There are various ways that you can protect yourself against manipulators.

Identify when You are a Victim

Everyone has a gut instinct that rears up when they are being used or misguided. Your gut instinct is very sound. You will know when you are a victim. The problem is, a lot of people ignore their instincts. You might ignore yours. You might think something like, "I'm just being paranoid" or "What could possibly go wrong if I hang out with this person?" You might think that the harm will be worth the benefits that you could get from knowing this person who gives you bad vibes. Maybe everyone else likes this guy, so you think that you are just being weird and you should like him too. Or maybe he is able to charm you and convince you that he is not so bad and over time you start to get over your initial bad vibes.

But vibes are not something that you should ever ignore. The minute your gut warns you about someone, listen. Your first impression of someone is never wrong. If you get a bad first impression, don't give the person a second chance. You know more about someone by just glancing at them than you would think. The human brain is amazingly powerful; you only are conscious of roughly ten percent of your brain, so there is a lot going on under the surface that you are not consciously aware of. Your brain is capable of reading people and determining the future far more than you realize.

So when you get that gut feeling, understand that your brain is working very hard and noticing things that you are not consciously aware of. The person that you get bad vibes may not be matching his body language to his words, or he may be acting oddly in ways that you can't detect easily. Listen to your gut!

If you are just not in touch with your gut at all, or if you have doubts about someone, you might want to consider looking at some other signs. You can identify a manipulator based on his actions and language choices. You can also tell by how you feel around this person. There are various clues that point out who someone really is and what his intentions are.

What Makes You Vulnerable

You may wonder why manipulators are attracted to you, especially if you have had multiple encounters with manipulative types. You may also wonder what you should change about yourself to avoid running into a manipulator in the future.

One thing that makes you vulnerable is being accepting of manipulative treatment and emotional abuse. If you were emotionally abused or repressed as a child, this type of treatment may seem normal to you. You don't know anything else. You don't how a healthy relationship is supposed to feel. So you accept the terrible treatment that others would not think of accepting. As a result, you are projecting a sense of vulnerability that draws manipulators from far away. The minute you begin to tolerate their treatment and keep them in your life, they gain power over you and choose to keep using you until they get what they want. Work on increasing your self-esteem and avoiding familiar patterns. If you get that eerie sense of déjà vu when you meet someone, you might want to avoid that person because he is probably reminding you of previous abusive patterns that you have been in.

Another thing that may make you vulnerable is neediness or weakness. If you are in a vulnerable time in life, you might be more open to manipulators. Manipulators can see that you are in need and they see it as an opportunity to offer you what you need in exchange of what they really want. They will use any opportunity to gain control over you, and when you are in a bad period of life, you basically hand them opportunities. You need to guard your heart and mind especially well when you are at a disadvantage. Be wary of extremely kind strangers or life savers. Not all heroes are good guys. Your heroes may help you, but they may have hidden intentions. Most people won't do something for free so watch out.

You may also be a target for manipulation if you have low self-esteem. Events in your life or your childhood may have stripped away your self-esteem and confidence. You may be emotionally vulnerable. So you want people who build up your ego. Manipulators can spot this and they will move in on you, working hard to please you and make you smile. They see a way into your mind through your bruised ego. Try to build your self-esteem by yourself and work on loving yourself.

But the unfortunate truth is, everyone is a potential victim. A manipulator will see the slightest opening in your psyche and move right in. Manipulators are skilled opportunists who shamelessly go after anyone that they can. If you fall prey to a manipulator, don't feel bad and don't blame yourself. It could happen to anyone. It is not your fault. The fact that you may become a victim is why you need to read this chapter and learn how to protect yourself.

Signs of a Manipulator

A manipulator is often incredibly superficial. This means that he looks good on the outside, but there is nothing to follow it up on the inside. He is shallow and lacks depth. Everything he does and says is fake, part of a façade that he erects to fool you. So beware of people who are incredibly charming and attractive when you first meet them. Get to know them before you start confiding in them or trusting them. Don't make a commitment or business deal until you are absolutely sure of yourself.

Another sign of a manipulator is that you feel compelled to confide in him or to do what he wants. You constantly find yourself saying yes when you want to say no. It's impossible to be yourself and to stand up for yourself. He has some sort of power over you that you can't resist. Unfortunately, this power is just a carefully woven web of manipulation, deception, and emotional harm. He will dump you the minute he gets all that he can from you, so don't stick around or make the mistake of thinking that this relationship will last. He does not care, no matter how well he pretends to. Get away from him before the relationship gets too harmful and he ruins your life.

You may also find yourself saying sorry all of the time. Your guilt eats you up. Every situation with this person seems like your fault. Even if he is at fault, he manages to twist things around so that you feel guilty. He will never take responsibility for anything that he does and he will always put everything on you. He can do what he wants, but he holds you to exacting standards and punishes you when you don't follow suit. He basically kills your self-esteem and causes you to hate yourself.

Finally, a manipulator is great at changing your mind. You might feel one way, but after talking with him, you feel a completely different way. He is able to change your mind and your way of thinking. Sometimes this may even be a good thing, as he makes you think more constructively or positively. But be wary of someone who has so much power over your moods and your thoughts.

What Manipulation Feels Like

Often, in the early stages of a manipulative or emotionally abusive relationship, you will feel amazing. Your manipulator will be an expert at making you feel good about yourself. He will flatter you and fuel your ego.

Some people out there will make you feel good because they genuinely love you. But it often takes times for such a relationship to build. If someone whom you barely know is suddenly super into you and trying to rush a relationship, become very wary. Don't let things move too quickly. Get to know the person first. Someone who wants you so badly right off of the bat is usually superficial and just trying to prime you into a victim. Don't fall for it. Normal people don't just jump into relationships or try to rush things. Normal people also don't start acting crazy about you in an unusually short period of time.

A manipulator will make you feel like there are butterflies in your stomach. You will strive to please him. Your biggest desire will be to make him smile. This is because he is already making you feel as if you owe him or as if you like him so much that you will work to please him. Beware of people who make you feel like a puppet. You should never want to bend over backwards for someone so urgently.

You need to have a sense of dignity and personal space and value in every relationship. If you don't, something is off.

You will also feel guilty about the smallest things. You may feel inadequate or guilty for not always pleasing this person every day. A sense of guilt about living or being you may haunt you. You may feel ashamed of who you are. These feelings may seem to come out of the blue, but this is just because you are with a super covert manipulator. Trust me, he is playing some serious games with your heart to inspire your guilt. These feelings are not random or spontaneous, but rather part of your manipulator's carefully crafted plan to hurt you. So you should become suspicious and understand that these feelings are not a normal element of a healthy relationship.

Your self-esteem will certainly dive when you spend time around a manipulator. Soon, your confidence will become riddled with holes. You will be poisoned with self-doubt and angst. This is not a good thing and you should not stay around someone who does this to you.

You also will probably start to feel crazy. You will wonder if you have an undiagnosed disorder or if you are falling apart at the seams. When you argue with this person, he will deny everything that he just said. He will call you nuts for arguing with him or claim that you are just making things up. In addition, he will invent elaborate stories and blame you for things that you never did, often so convincingly that you start to believe that you did what he claims. He will also challenge your perception of reality, lie through his teeth, and make you question yourself constantly. All of these things combined will tear at your self-esteem and consciousness, making you question your sanity. Manipulators can actually rewire the neurons of your brain and do permanent damage to your mental health and personality, so you should not stick around.

One great piece of advice is that if you feel the need to record someone during arguments because he denies what he says later and makes you feel crazy, then you are in an emotionally abusive relationship and you should leave now. You are not crazy. This person is just gaslighting you.

What to Do when Someone is Manipulating You

The simplest piece of advice on how to deal with a manipulator is to just up and leave. If you can do this, great. You should immediately. There will be no good to come from this relationship, so why stay around and get hurt?

But this advice is often easier said than done. There are some situations where you cannot escape a manipulator and his traps. For instance, you might have to work with a manipulator and you can't just quit your job, or you don't want to. Or you might have a manipulative family member and you can't cut him off or you will lose all of your family. You may feel trapped and unable to leave for various reasons, such as financial reasons. Maybe you have kids with the manipulator and must speak to him or her for the rest of your life regarding the children. Co-parenting doesn't automatically end when your children turn eighteen; sometimes, you have to continue a relationship with the father or mother well into your children's' adult lives, and you must be around each other for your children's weddings, graduations, grandchildren, etc. Or maybe there is a manipulative friend in your group whom everyone else likes. There are countless reasons why you may be stuck with a manipulator in your life. Leaving is not always a viable option.

That is OK. Because you can easily handle manipulators.

The first step is to limit contact with the person. Avoid him as much as you reasonably can. Limiting contact allows him less time to toy with your mind. Try to add sources of joy to your life so that you can escape his negativity and start to feed your soul. Take some time to yourself so that you can recover from the harm that comes with interactions with this monster.

The second step is to plan your escape. Maybe you can't escape now. But if you develop a plan and watch out for opportunities to escape this person, you can start to prepare yourself for freedom. An end may be in sight. Make it a goal to leave this person behind in life as soon as possible. Take steps toward your goal each day. Only in a few cases can you never, ever escape a manipulator, so if you stick to your plan to get away, you will eventually. Life changes and people move on. You won't be trapped in this situation forever. Keep your chin up and keep your eyes on the end goal.

The third step is to avoid buying into his games. Say he tries to gaslight you. Don't start arguing with him, crying, acting out in anger, or recording him to prove that you are right. Just shrug and say, "OK." He won't like how easily he won the game because he likes the fight and he likes upsetting you. Don't ever show him that he upset you, because that is how he truly wins. Instead, swallow your pride and tell him that he is right. He will soon get bored and move on to his next victim. Then you won't have to deal with him anymore.

The fourth step is to avoid doing what he really wants. You might let him win arguments, but you don't have to do what he tells you. Say he tries getting you to break up with someone. You can tell him that he's right and you will break up with this person – but then never do. It will drive him crazy that he doesn't have control over you. He will hate that you do whatever you want. Or let's use another example: he decides to pout and embarrass you at a party so that you'll leave early and do what he wants. Just ignore him with a smile on your face. Don't leave the party until you are good and ready. You can even keep telling him, "Yes, we'll leave!" but then don't. Being nice rather than combative will disarm him and keep him from fighting you, while you continue to do what you want and not what he wants.

He might try to hurt you to punish you for not doing what he wants. He might discredit you or tell you things that deeply wound you. Don't let him get to you. Determine to move on and repair the damage. Start working on recovery right away. Being resilient like this will repel him. He will see that you are not an easy victim and he will move on to someone who is. When he starts picking at you, trying to trigger your anger or sadness, just ignore it or respond to him nicely and don't fall for the trap. Try to prove to others that you didn't do what he claims as well.

Another tactic he will use is making you seem crazy to others. If you keep a cool head and don't follow his games or his sick reasoning, you will avoid appearing crazy to others. Be as innocent as you can be. Keep an impeccable reputation and be nice to others. Eventually, people will see the truth. Even if your reputation is already damaged, you can still mitigate the damage by being the best version of yourself possible. You will win over some people at least, and kill his goal of making you look terrible.

Block Someone's Access to Your Mind

Your mind is more vulnerable than you think. Everyone is sensitive to suggestion, so you can easily fall prey to manipulators without meaning to. But you also have more power over your own mind than you think. You can guard your mind and block the attempts of manipulators.

The best way to block your mind is to gain a healthy sense of self-love and self-confidence. If you believe in yourself, you won't let others mess with your sense of self-worth and happiness. You won't fall for the tricks and self-esteem games of manipulators. Talk to yourself nicely, as if you are your own best friend. Treat yourself to nice things or spa trips or other experiences. Tend to your needs as a priority and don't feel bad about being selfish sometimes. You should come first. Your needs matter and you matter. Remember this always.

A lot of people have low self-esteem and feel bad about taking care of themselves, which makes them vulnerable to cutthroat manipulators and con artists.

Another way is to whip out a recording device or start writing down what someone says to you. You should use this tactic with people who often try to gaslight you. Do it with a smile on your face. Say, "We have often had miscommunication in the past, so I want to make sure that I catch exactly what you say for later." This will make a manipulator incredibly nervous. But if you're nice about it, you can avoid a fight and disarm him.

Having witnesses around is also a good idea. He will be less likely to attack your mind with other people around. Always keep yourself armed with friends. Don't go anywhere alone with him. If you find yourself alone with him, be sure to leave at the first opportunity.

You should carefully and closely guard your personal business. Don't reveal too much to many people. Get to know someone really well and measure his sincerity over time based on how he treats others before you start to reveal things like what you love, what you hate, or what you are guilty about. Trust is precious and you shouldn't trust many people, especially those who seem very trustworthy when you first meet them. Manipulators can fool you so don't make hasty judgments about someone's good character.

When someone tries to mess with your mind, just tell them with a smile, "Don't do that." He will try to deny doing anything wrong and may even call you crazy. Just don't respond to those antagonistic efforts. You called him out, he knows that what he was doing was wrong, and now you can move on with your day. Soon he will realize that he can't get to you or make you doubt yourself.

You can also turn the tables on someone by doing the opposite of what he wants. For instance, if he tries to bring you down, just tell him that you prefer to stay positive and try to inspire him to stay positive too. If he tries to make you doubt yourself, tell him that you are comfortable with who you are. If he wants to complain and ruin something, just tell him that you are actually having a nice time and he should try to enjoy himself too. Don't fight him, but don't do what he wants either. This will drive him crazy and eventually make him back down. You may even make a positive difference in his attitude. Not all manipulators mean to be terrible people; many of them simply don't know how to get what they want in healthy ways.

When someone tries to tear you down by being insulting, you can smile and say, "Wow, I never thought about myself like that. But we all have flaws. I can definitely understand things from your perspective, too." He will be shocked and disarmed that he can't get to you. Your willingness to blithely accept what he says without getting combative will throw him off.

Set an example by being a good person to yourself and to others. This will enable you to block a lot of manipulation attempts. Manipulators simply won't be able to tarnish your reputation or bring you down.

They won't be able to get a rise out of you or make you appear crazy when they goad you to desperate acts of anger.

Use Manipulation Back on Someone

One great trick is to use manipulation on someone who is manipulating you. Turn the tables on them. Make their plans fail as you covertly work to undermine their goals in manipulating you. Pretend to do what they want, and secretly mess up the whole plan. Or use their manipulation as means to get what you really want. You may or may not choose to be covert about the whole thing. It depends on how much you want to annoy or punish the person.

There are countless ways to do this. You need to observe the situation and plan accordingly. Use the tactics you learned throughout the previous chapters to find a way to covertly manipulate this person into doing what you want, while letting him think that he is getting his way with you.

some examples of people who used it during the history

Here are a few examples of things that you can do:

Someone immature in your office is spreading rumors about you. When you hear these rumors about yourself, laugh and say, "That's funny, coming from him." When the other person asks why you say that, start a rumor of your own. Tell people how they can't believe anything he says because of something ugly from his own past. Dig up some dirt on him and expose him for who he really is, or make up something that everyone will believe.

Your mother-in-law likes to make you feel guilty so that you bring the grandkids over more often. She uses various tactics to make you feel like dirt and is over-involved in your relationship with her child. Confronting her is not an option because she will blow up at you and cause problems in your marriage. So you can bring the kids over, but you make the visit as unbearable as possible. Don't discipline the children and let them wreak havoc in her house. Feed them tons of sugar before the visit so that they are extremely naughty and hyper. Maybe bring them as late as possible, when she is too tired to be patient and they are tired too so they whine and throw tantrums. If you go out to eat, take them somewhere that they hate so that they complain, cry, and refuse to eat. She won't want them to come over as much. She may also eventually lose her temper and discipline them harshly, which you can use as an excuse to make your spouse mad at her and cause a rift in the relationship so that you don't have to tolerate her demands anymore.

A manipulative friend likes to hurt you with little digs. "You have such pretty hair today for once!" is an example of the barbed insults that she will throw at you to hurt you. Instead of confronting her directly, you can pull the same trick. Smile at her and say things like, "Thanks! Your hair could use work, though. You should try my stylist." Hurt her right back but don't do it obviously.

Someone wants to ruin a party so that everyone will pay attention to her and do what she wants. So you let her ruin the party. Pay attention to her. But turn it into negative attention. Make everyone start to criticize her. Embarrass her with hurtful jokes about herself. She will think that you are giving her what she wants – until you're not. She will quickly learn not to mess with you because you have even better ammo.

You notice that a businessman is trying to "yes frame" you by asking you questions with yes answers. So turn it around by only saying no. Or start asking him your own line of questions to throw him off. It will kill the sale and help you avoid a regrettable purchase.

These are just some of many examples of how you can turn manipulation around on someone. You need to analyze the situation and find out how you can play games right back.

Chapter 3: Human Behavior and Manipulation

Once you have gotten a decent read on a person, the next step to mastering your environment and analyzing your potential in each situation is learning how to manipulate another person's feelings and reactions through more subtle cues, both verbal and non-verbal. This will create an environment where your suggestions can thrive.

Don't beat yourself up for thinking outside the box when it comes to analyzing and influencing people. While some people might call it manipulation, you can simply tell them that you are extremely persuasive. What's more, there is nothing to say that the person you are influencing wasn't waiting for an excuse to move forward in the direction you suggested anyway. It is your creativity in constructing a good plan or formula that turns resistance into compliance.

Manipulation Basics

The art of manipulation lies in the engrained principals of protecting and nourishing other people, both of which forms a quick emotional bond. It is important to keep in mind that the stronger the emotion you can make another person feel, the easier it will be to bend them to your will. Emotion is what controls the world, gain control over your own, practice reading people, and learn how to persuade and analyze and you will be well on your way to manipulating others successfully.

Besides emotion, successful manipulation is all about the imbalance of power. There may be times when getting what you want from another person means using the home court advantage which means keeping the person in an environment in which you have primary control. This includes your home, car, office, or even your side of town. This makes it harder for your target to do things such as dodge a conversation or even make a decision that they think might hurt your feelings.

While it may seem surprising, letting another person dominate the conversation is a good thing when you want to have the upper hand with them. You can establish their underlying weaknesses and their strengths by listening to their stories and throwing in a few questions from time to time, which will also ingratiate you to them further as it makes you seem as though you are supremely interested in what they have to say. You aren't going to want to let the conversation feel one sided, however, which means you will want to tell them enough about your situation to make them feel comfortable while at the same time withholding any information that would weaken your standpoint or that could be contorted to mean something else. Don't be afraid to lie to protect any weaknesses in your argument.

If someone is pushing you for more than they need, you can use a humble tone, and explain that there are things about you no one would understand, or that you aren't interesting enough to warrant talking about. This will make them curious, and it will also make them a little nurturing, which is where you can snag them. This is known as flipping the script and it can be a very effective technique when used selectively.

If you have to, speak about facts and statistics. Ramble about as many as you can to be a bit overwhelming. At this time, you need to show interest on their part but establish that if you are to go along with whatever they are suggesting, then you are going to have your own rules. Depending on the situation you are currently in, this may be enough for them to "decide" to complete the task in question for you or to give in to your suggestion because it is easier than going along with your stipulations.

Another way to manipulate a person is to change the modulation of your voice. If you are trying to intimidate a person, you will want to be loud. If you are seeking sympathy, lose the loud tone for a depressed, defeated tone instead. Most people are inclined to help a person who is feeling down. Now that you have their sympathy, ask for something. Suggest what you want in a way that seems impossible to achieve. Wait for their response, which should be some variation of, "I want to help you." Some people will want to offer up advice as a way to soothe you. To avoid losing control of the situation you will need to consider their advice and find a reason that their logic is faulty to ensure things remain under your control.

Manipulation tools for specific situations

A key to pulling off any form of manipulation is to see what drives the person you are dealing with. For example, is it a religion? If so, you would need to focus on their devotion and find a creative way to get your point across using their religion. It is a good way to reinforce their opinion of themselves which is most likely that they are godly and intelligent. As long as you focus on their utopian visions and aspirations, you will find this technique to be very effective.

Another tool that is useful from time to time is sarcasm. It allows you to express your discontent with someone while maintaining a doorway out as if you were just joking. But be cautious, as sarcasm can be insulting and hurtful if misused. After you have been given the chance to vent, turn it around to the sarcastic "what if." This allows the person to hear your opinion, and it comes across like you are just defeated. Now they can save you. When they offer their help, humbly tell them it is not their responsibility, but that you do need their support. It is helpful to add, "What would I do without you?"

You must keep in mind that you are being manipulated every day. The news, media, and those in power all deploy tactics to keep your attention or threaten your security for non-compliance. You are bombarded with images and stories that tug at your heart, anger your soul, and move you either into action or into seclusion. Just seeing how easily you can have the same effect on a person, will allow you to recognize when it is being done to you. Awareness is life changing. It is at this moment that you realize you have tried conventional methods of persuasion, being genuine and truly caring. Previously, you got nothing in return, but you will from now on.

Be creative

You will need to focus on your creativity for these manipulative tactics. Your goal is to transform someone's reality and alter their beliefs. Every situation is different which means you will need to be creative and think on your feet. You must observe the cues a person is giving you. You must observe their reactions to you and to others, as these can be very telling. Sometimes, just watching your target interact with others can give you more insight on how to manipulate them.

For example, if you see how a coworker reacted to a customer, you can use that to make them feel justified by adding your opinion as an out to explain how they reacted. They will repeat the excuse you provided them. This can be used against them later. If you are trying to get them to do something for you, just point out how they overreacted to that customer which should shame them into following your suggestion. They should act in the way you suggest to minimize their past actions.

Sometimes all you have to do is create an image. Think of a spin on something that would suggest the person you are dealing with is a victim. Encourage them to see how others have been unappreciative and lazy compared to them. Suggest a course of action and reap the benefits.

If you are dying to know what someone feels about a situation, for example in politics or religion, make up a story that you read on the internet that is sure to rile them up. Sit back and watch their reaction and start agreeing with them. Be sure to add your perspective to draw them out of the shocking story into your plan. You might just be harvesting information to keep a profile on someone who is a threat to your vision of success. Building your profile, you will be able to understand their weakness in most situations.

Take your time

You can be sure to pay special attention to their strengths and find ways to undermine them. Don't take it so far as to where others observing can figure out what your intentions are, and instead always take the high road in public so that at the end of the day, most people will only ever see the public face you decide to show them.

Keep in mind that everyone really just wants to be happy which means they seek to have understanding and supportive people around them. They think it is rare for someone to take an interest in them without wanting something in return. This is where patience becomes your ally. You cannot really act like someone has to be available at a moment's notice. Anyone can figure out that you have selfish motives if you display this impatient tendency. It might be killing you to lie in wait for the perfect opportunity, but it would kill you more to be seen as a fake. So, wait. Even encourage them to ask others about the situation. Once you have proven that you are only worried about them or want to see them succeed, then you can wiggle into their mind with subtle manipulation.

While playing on the heartstrings of another, you weaken their response. You cannot simply ignore that they might say no to your request or idea. You have to come across as sincere in trying to help or care about them. Find a way to make their "no" seem unreasonable without saying it directly. You will have to point out that if someone else acted like they did, with their closed mind, they would see it as being stubborn or pig-headed. Let them know that the brain has a chemical response to doing something new and brave. Tell them that the brain lights up like a Christmas tree when changes are occurring.

The bottom line is that there is potential in manipulation. It is a creative process. It takes a little planning and observing. But if mastered, it can change your life. You will feel powerful every day. You will start to see every rejection as a canvas. It is your starting point. A word for word or gesture by gesture guarantee that you are in control.

Self- preservation is an important aspect of manipulation. You do not want to be seen as a manipulator. You want to be known as the neutral person who sees all sides but uses logic to decide why your decision is more valid. Maintain a solid reputation for being thoughtful and people will seek your opinion often. This is an advantage from the start. In a new group of people, you can find a way to agree with everyone, and make a statement that you were always taught to show respect and think of all sides before making a decision. This could have the others taking your point into consideration just because you were willing to do this for them. This becomes your thoughtful reputation.

There are many forms of manipulation which actually can benefit you and your target. You cannot feel guilty for taking drastic measures to appeal to their dark psychosis. It is for everyone and can hardly be avoided. It is time for you to recognize the signs of it happening to you and take control of the situation. Start to think that when a person says no, they are being self-destructive. They will need you to help them think for themselves. In the end, they might even thank you for your help, as if they were just struggling until you came along with a solution. After you accomplish your goal, make a statement about how much calmer and happier they seem now that they have tried new things as it reinforces your behavior.

As you by now know, Neuro-linguistic Programming (or NLP) was founded on the theory and premise that people process everything through neurological means, our language, and programming deigned from life experiences. NLP practitioners believe that since the neurological system regulated overall bodily functions, and that language determines how we communicate with others, the two aspects go together specifically to dictate how we are programmed, or how we behave, and that these programmed behaviors can be altered both within ourselves, but used to persuade other individuals as well.

NLP modeling is the process of reconstructing superiority. We can model all human behaviors by mastering the beliefs, physiology, and the specific thought methods that trigger the ability or behavior. It is about achieving a specific result from another person by learning how that other person goes about their own individual way of thinking. Following NLP models require that manipulators be able to transfer what the "experts" think they know, and shifting that knowledge into everyday applications for a manipulators own designs. Next, we will go over a couple of popular NLP models, and give examples of how to follow them to become aware of NLP tactics that manipulators can use to gain control over others.

The Milton Model

The Milton Model is a useful form of NLP that uses language to induce and maintain hypnotic states. There are three main aspects of the Milton model: rapport, overloading tactics, and finally, indirect interpretation.

In consideration of the first step of building rapport, observation skills need to be honed specifically to better build the bond or relationship that a manipulator desires to achieve. Taking note of eye movements, and the way an individual tilts the head or ears, is an important task manipulators work on to begin building rapport as it indicates to exactly how the person's mind works to store information. If you notice another individual using more eye cues, making statements like "I see", that leads the other person to subconsciously feel as though you are similar. Comments that start with "I hear" geared towards an individual who uses physical cues that indicate they are more auditory allow for the other party to feel "heard" by the manipulator, and again, evoke a feeling of similarity between the manipulator and their mark. By noticing and duplicating the way in which another individual communicates, they are immediately giving the other party signals that both of them are a "we" who see things in the same light. Manipulators will often employ observation and begin to mirror another's way of speaking and physical mannerisms to help them build rapport faster. Without being obvious, manipulators will slowly begin to mirror the other party's physical stance or posture, begin cautious not make fast or immediate changes to their own stance. As initial communication unfolds, manipulators will then begin to also use the same speaking tone and volume as the other person does. Even beginning to match their breathing patterns to the target's own will create a sense of cohesiveness. Another way manipulators build rapport is to find a commonality between themselves and the other person, even if it is miniscule or under false pretense on their part. The goal of the master manipulator is to build a relationship out of thin air, being careful not to commit to any common experience that can be disproved later and break trust. Manipulators will know they have successfully built rapport with another person by then testing them. If the target is speaking slowly, they will begin to do the same, and then slowly begin to increase the pace of their speech pattern. If the individual in question matches the manipulators pace in return, rapport has been established. Another way manipulators will often test to determine if the rapport has been built successfully is by paying close attention to the reactions to what they say that the other person shows. Manipulators are always assessing, and considering questions like: "Are the responses and facial reactions they wanted to illicit in others being conveyed back to them effectively?" If so, the manipulator knows that they are now in.

The second aspect of the Milton model, referred to as overloading is not to say that the manipulator is overloading the person they wish to perform NLP techniques on, but rather that they are overloading the other person's conscious with vague language to help access their subconscious mind. One of the easiest techniques Milton described was to use a subtle conversational hypnotic tactic often referred to as the double bind. The double bind gives the appearance of two choices, answers, or outcomes, but either response gives the manipulator the desired outcome. When people assume they have a choice between one thing or another, they are more likely to cooperate and focus on the two choices before them. The presupposition of only two choices is accepted unconsciously, and very rarely will the person choose outside of the two options given, despite the obvious fact that there is always another choice. Consider when dining out, the waiter will ask "will you be paying with cash or would you like to use your card?" The presupposition is that you are not going to try and break the law, and of course you are paying for your meal. But, what choice in the matter are you really being given? None. You are paying for your meal. It is a perfect example of a double binding question.

Now that presuppositions have been mentioned, it should be understood that these are also very effective modes of altering another's thoughts in an almost imperceivably way. Presuppositions are the things stated that are assumed in conversation, whether they truly are or you wish them to be so. Statements like "So, are you going to attend the party before or after the kids go to sleep?", or "Will you be finishing that up today or tomorrow morning?", are good examples of presupposing statements. Was the individual given a choice to not attend the party at all, or not finishing up whatever task was asked about? No. They were given the option of when they were going to do what you wanted them to do.

There are many other techniques Milton discussed regarding this second step, including asking tag questions, or statements that include a question at the end, using language that is ambiguous in nature to confuse the mind, using utilization to take advantage of your intentions, or using unspecified verbs during a conversation all help a manipulator confuse the conscious mind and allow the other person to be open to subliminal suggestions they want to influence on their targets.

The third facet of Milton's model is to use metaphoric speaking to leave what they are saying open to interpretation by the other party. Whether using a well-known metaphor, or one of their own creation, manipulators make sure that the metaphor is relative to the conversation or issue at hand. This will help the other individual relate the current communication to another instance, and leave them using more of their subconscious brain that they would in normal conversation. Tapping into the subconscious mind in one of the ultimate goals of the master manipulator.

Other NLP Tactics

Sometimes, the best way for a manipulator to get what you want is to ask the right question at the right time. Or even better, why not frame the question in the correct way to get the right, or their desired, response to begin with? A very useful technique for manipulators is to use the subliminal persuasion technique of conversational hypnosis to basically tell the other person what they want the answer to be, then ask the question in such a way that their mark will obviously sway their answer to what they think is the "correct" response. By using this skill, manipulators don't have to literally say out loud what they want to hear from others, because doing so could cause the other person to retaliate or refuse. When this maneuver is done properly, the person the manipulator wishes to persuade thinks they are the one who has come up with the correct response all on their own. And how could anyone deny or refute something they themselves have thought up? A great example of this would be if a manipulator were trying to convince someone way out of their league on a date. The manipulator may start the interaction as follows:

"I know I am probably not your type at all, nor you mine, but isn't the same old so boring? Aren't you ready to try something different too?"

This tactic is very useful, and by throwing in an acknowledgement that they aren't necessarily the archetype of the other person's typical idea of dating material, but also that they aren't their norm either, the manipulator is leveling the playing field to their advantage. The target or mark will have no idea what the manipulators type is, all they know is that they aren't it. Interesting how someone out of your league can quickly begin to wonder what league they themselves are really in, isn't it?

Learning Neuro-Logical Levels

Probably the most helpful tool for a manipulator in the NLP arsenal is learning and understanding the Neuro-Logical Levels model. This model maps people and their distinctive personalities into six different groupings based on three aspects: thinking, feeling, and actions. Utilizing this model allows manipulators to comprehend in a clear and organized method what drives another person. The Neuro-logical levels model can be assessed while actively communicating with another person, and is broken down in the following way by the manipulator:

Identity: What is the other person's self-esteem level? Are they happy with their image, both how they see themselves and how others perceive them? How do you identify with this person? Do you both have families?

Environment: Where are you now, and how is the other person positively or negatively responding to the current surroundings?

Behavior: How is this person acting? What good or positive behavioral tendencies are you noticing? Are there any negative behaviors being exhibited, and if so, why? Facial expressions, posture, nonverbal cues, all need to be taken into consideration.

Skills: What skills does this person have as it relates to the situation or interaction? What skills are they lacking? Are they aware of any skills they are lacking in or anything they excel at?

Beliefs: What are their beliefs and values that they hold dear? Do any of these core belief systems help or hinder this person? Do they align with my own values, or is there a way to align them with mine?

Mission: What is this person's motivation? Where are they trying to get in life? What are their hopes, their contributions, what is the central vision or goal they have for themselves?

By using this model and developing their ability to hone in on these questions and the answers given by their targets, the manipulator is learning how to understand and communicate to their advantage at a much faster pace. This structured way of observing and analyzing another person while they are communicating will further enable the manipulator to interact easily with many different types of individuals successfully, as they can discover what makes other people tick, and then they use it to help them manipulate the interaction.

How Manipulative Behavior Develops

If you can understand individuals by their behaviors, then you will never be tricked by their words. Keep in mind that what an individual says and does are two separate things. Since manipulative individuals may "woo" you with their words of kindness, ensure they actually live up to their words and that it is not just an empty shell for a trap.

If a manipulative individual put as much exertion into being a decent individual as they do into professing to be one, they could be a trustworthy individual. Remember, even though the warnings we share throughout the book, manipulation doesn't always have to be a bad thing. Don't mistake someone's attempt at positive influence as them trying to manipulate you.

If we comprehended from the earliest starting point that an individual isn't who they appear to be and merely is taking cover behind an exterior of what seems, by all accounts, to be socially satisfactory conduct, at that point we would be careful about engaging with them.

Constantly inspect what you accept. We don't do this enough. As life advances, our convictions and frames of mind may change, and we have to know how these changing thoughts influence us.

Understanding the root of manipulation is the best way to grasp what it is and how it can affect you. It is easy to think that those who are manipulators are just bad and selfish people. You can ignore these individuals and keep them out of your life, but we have to remember to really accept the truth about these types of people. They can seem bad, but they will still be present in our lives, and understanding their complexities will help us the most in the end.

Motivations and Intention

Manipulation starts with motivation and intention. All manipulation is a product of someone attempting to get what she desires. The issue is that there is a more intense focus on getting that at all costs rather than getting it practically. We have a sense of urgency sometimes and feel our needs will not be met if we aren't pushing people to give us what we want. We all have different desires and hopes, and a manipulator is someone who simply goes about getting these things in the wrong way.

Manipulation can sometimes start in childhood. If you weren't properly taught to express your feelings or share the things that you want, then it can be hard to know how to get them, or to satisfy those feelings. We can start from an early age trying to twist reality and shape it to help us fulfill our needs. It is a quick fix sometimes to influence someone else to do what you want rather than doing it the hard way yourself. We can confuse wanting to be close with someone for wanting to control them, so we will take mistaken actions trying to fulfill that inner need.

There is an important distinction between manipulation, inspiration, and motivation that we have to make ourselves aware of. As someone on the road to becoming persuasive, it's important to understand the difference between the motives of those who are trying to persuade or influence and the motives of the people who intentionally try to manipulate.

Persuasive motivation takes place when a person is considerate of the work that needs to be done and the person as well. Manipulation comes in when the individual is only concerned with the actual work that needs to be done, not the person who would be doing it. When an individual is concerned with only making money for her business, not caring how she might be exploiting her workers, using fear tactics to keep them working and underpaying them, she is operating in a manipulative fashion.

Persuasive motivation takes place when a person is compassionate for the person whom they are influencing. Manipulation comes from a desire for pride and power over another person. If someone is trying to get you to quit drinking because you have a problem that has led to alcoholism, they are motivated to help you. If a husband wants his wife to stop drinking because he doesn't like when his wife goes out to wine tasting with friends, then this is manipulation.

Persuasive motivation is based in the truth and actual, substantial honesty. Manipulation is only concerned with outward appearances. If someone is trying to encourage you to lose weight after a heart attack, this is motivation. If someone is trying to encourage you to lose weight because your stomach doesn't look flat in a bikini, but your health is completely fine, this would be manipulation.

Persuasive motivation actually cares about the other person and is concerned with their needs and desires. Manipulation is only grounded in fulfillment for the self that can be achieved with or without hurting people–it is not concerned with others.

Leaders should consistently self-reflect to evaluate their movites and to guarantee they are genuinely persuading—not controlling. If you are guilty of controlling, of endeavoring to control individuals or not thinking about those you lead, you aren't driving success.

Our Thoughts and Feelings

Manipulators are individuals who routinely take part in shrewd, ascertaining, and scheming conduct. Master manipulators like this are often called Machiavellians or High Machs. On the other hand, the label Low Mach implies that one's cunning inclinations fall inside the usual range. While Low Machs can possibly take part in deceptive conduct, they incline toward not swindling and manipulating, except for when they see such behavior is needed or of importance.

For what reason are people wired to be High Machs? Does a fundamental identity issue cause the conduct? Assuming this is the case, is it possible to deal with the issue at hand? To put it plainly, no.

Identity issues don't transform individuals into High Machs. Machiavellianism is an inherited quality, presumably then worsened by an individual's social and family conditions. Cunning predispositions exist separate from any identity issue that an individual may have. However, we should not ignore identity issues completely.

Different identity issues can create tension, alarm, dejection, separation, craziness, happiness and other states of mind which may trigger aggressive responses. When somebody routinely deludes and uses others to prove their own points, that individual may develop the label—self-assigned or otherwise—of a manipulator.

Being under constant stress from an identity issue does not give terrible conduct a free pass. We have a decision to make before we act, and we are in charge of our behavior. Keeping this in mind, some individuals with specific identity issues may be inclined to fall back on manipulative conduct as a way of persevering and dealing with stress.

Aside from these underlying mental issues, such as antisocial personality disorder, borderline personality disorder, bipolar disorder, and obsessive-compulsive disorder, there are certain thoughts and feelings that will commonly drive someone to become a master manipulator.

The first feeling that might drive manipulation is fear. As soon as our brains sense that we might not be getting the exact thing that we feel we need, then we can end up becoming severely dependent on controlling others to fulfill that desire.

The fear of being alone can lead to someone manipulating multiple people in their lives in order to ensure that person will stick around. When we are fearful of losing the things we have, like money and material objects, it can cause us to manipulate, often in the workplace, to get what we want and ensure we stay in a higher position.

This feeling of fear and the desperate desire to alleviate that anxiety is validated by the thought that we are not good enough to get what we want on our own. Manipulators and those who struggle with controlling others are doing so because they usually have low self-esteem that tells them that they are not good enough and need to look to others to gain control and motivation.

Manipulators can also have strong feelings of desire. They will desperately want some things and think that the only way they can get these is if they manipulate others. Someone might desperately desire the admiration of others, so they can manipulate perspectives to make them seem more desirable than in reality.

The reason that many manipulators have this behavior is because they are not aware of the actual things that they want and allow their emotions to be the biggest driver in their decisions surrounding their life.

Rather than being conscious of the things that they actually want and how to properly achieve these things without hurting others, they will act from one moment to the next, having no logical plans for the best way to actually get what they want.

The Science of Manipulation

As humans, we are concerned most with preserving ourselves. Whether this is by getting shelter, food, rest, or whatever else fulfills our most primitive instincts, this is what drives our mind at the very root of it all. Some people will understand this and practice self-control, even when their animalistic behaviors are in the driver's seat. However, others will not realize this and instead think that the thing they want the most is the answer to all their problems.

We start to create certain expectations about the world, as well. Maybe you have an idea in your head of what you want in the future, and this seems like the perfect answer to everything. As most of us know, nothing will ever turn out the way we think, and little actually ever feels the way we think it will be when predicting it.

Still, there are some days where you expect to have a perfect plan of what the day will look like. When things go wrong, it can lead to manipulative tactics to try and achieve that desired outcome. When things don't go the way we planned, our brains can start to panic. We worry that if one thing doesn't happen, that means all other things we were hoping for won't either, and we can take some extreme measures to try and fulfill those desires.

It is not that we manipulate because our brains are giving us what is needed. Manipulation comes from simply thinking that doing so will give us what we **think** we need, not what will actually help us in the long run. When you are hungry, you are hungry in that moment, even if you know that you are going to eat in an hour. You don't just get to shut off that feeling of hunger. Your body doesn't care about time. It cares about what it needs in that moment.

Manipulators are concerned with filling their needs in the moment. If we all sat down and really thought through all the challenging feelings that we have, then most relationships would be in a much better place. Instead, our animalistic brains are making us act in ways that drive us towards getting only what we want in that moment.

Though it is a scientific thing that happens in the moment, long-term manipulation is simply a pattern of this kind of thought process. It becomes a habitual way of thinking for many people, and our brains accept this as the way to actually get the things that we want, no matter who might get harmed along the way.

How Manipulators Step In

All of this may sound simple. You might start to think of a manipulator as an evil villain who doesn't care if they hurt others to get what they want. You start to think of villains, such as Cruella de Ville who might kill puppies just to get a fancy fur coat. So how, then, are manipulators able to step into our lives? The implications of this question are great since this kind of manipulation happens on both an individual level and a societal one, as well. And our society has become used to it.

The idea of what manipulation is can seem evil and obvious, but what actually happens is that it starts small and expands into a confusing web of inflated stories, misunderstandings, and others doing whatever they can to convince you of the things they want you to believe.

Manipulation starts with the person who plans on taking advantage of others. They will first go through something that has taught them that manipulating others is the way to get the things that they want. Next, they will find their victim. This will usually be a more compassionate person and someone who has shown love and empathy to them. A manipulator will rarely start a relationship right away with another manipulator.

From there, they will form a close bond, making the other person feel special and unique. Next, they will start to slowly show signs of control, but this will usually be out of "love," or so they make it seem.

Next, they will start to actually control what you do, and when resistance is shown, the manipulator will try even harder to make you believe that you are unable to trust yourself.

After that, the other person usually becomes aware of the manipulation and leaves, or they will not recognize what is happening and fall deeper into the lies building up around them.

This cycle is hard to break, but it needs to be done. It is not fair for one person to take advantage of another. We all help each other, and there are some things that we need from others, like love, financial help, or simply emotional support. These are all things that should be given clearly and consensually, not something to be manipulated out of them.

Chapter 4: Emotional Intelligence and Manipulation

Emotional intelligence is about self-awareness, self-management, and relationship management. It's about understanding yourself and having the ability to manage your emotions, plus your response to those emotions.

However, although emotional intelligence can be learned, it isn't something you learn in a weekend program and be "covered" for the others of your life. That is a lifelong learning skill, that needs to be practiced and improved on throughout life.

To consider yourself emotionally intelligent, you should try to build up empathy which can make it easy to connect with others and know how they feel. Empathetic people are those people who are genuinely thinking about others and who readily offer support and help to those who require it. Not everyone can place themselves in other folks' shoes and try to understand their motives, which explains why empathy can be such a very important skill.

For this very reason, developing emotional intelligence should come easily to a person who is a natural empath or a people person. Others can find out about it in a course or from a created book, but as with most other abilities, to be proficient at it, you need to practice and apply emotional intelligence to as much situations as possible.

However, having high empathy is not easy. You need to be willing to listen in to various other person's feelings and attitude, to try and understand their behavior, to pay attention without judgment, etc. Not everyone can do this, which explains why many believe that empathy is not a skill, but a natural gift.

In other words, emotionally intelligent people are not empathic only once it suits them, but all the time. This is probably why there are very few extremely empathic people around, although it's no secret that empathy could be faked, either to influence somebody or for self-promotion.

Emotional Intelligence

Emotional intelligence (also referred to as emotional quotient or EQ) refers to your developed capacity to identify, appreciate, control, and use emotions to advantage yourself as well as others confidently. This definition could be split into four basic categories:

- Recognition: To become alert to your own emotions also to recognize your relationship with them.
- Appreciation: This can be the most difficult aspect to master since you must figure out how to appreciate your emotions for what they are. Only one time you accept them and find a genuine appreciation for them is it possible to move on to control them in a healthy manner.

- Control: Many people confuse this factor with suppression of emotion. To suppress them is indeed a kind of control nonetheless it is forced and only short-term. Suppression leaves you more hurt and susceptible to eruption over time. The purpose here is to allow emotions to release in a controlled way so that they look for a healthy release beneficial to you as well as your interactions.

- Confidence: The final aspect of EQ where you can effectively use your emotions in conversation to relieve tension, pull through challenging conditions, resolve squabbles & dissensions, and be empathetic to others.

Consequently, a strongly developed sense of emotional intelligence can help you establish and comprehend momentous and emotional episodes in the lives of those around you. At the smallest amount, emotional cleverness equips you having the ability to know your emotions, this is of these feelings, and the potential results your emotions have on those around you. The theory concept here is based on understanding and managing your emotions.

It is important to realize that emotional intelligence is a learned skill and not necessarily a birthright. To gain this skill, you have to train yourself. The good news is that you can sufficiently learn it anytime in your life, which is also why there is no need a good reason to lack this essential skill!

Although most people generally know what emotions are, it is important to first define and understand exactly what is being referred to throughout this written publication.

What Are Emotions?

There are varied definitions of emotions plus some existing literature attempts to compare emotions with feelings in a bid to justify which of both precedes the other. Taking all information and viewpoints into consideration, we can define emotions on three different levels.

- Physically: Feelings are reactions from the brain's subcortical sections in response to stimuli. These reactions generate biochemical responses within your body thus changing one's physical condition. They can in turn compel one to action on any matter that stirs the emotions in the threatening or enjoyable way. For this reason, they are seen as part of human survival instincts also.

- Mentally: Emotions are normal responses that provide rise to certain thoughts and circumstances of the mind, changing one's state of mind with regards to the stimuli. For this reason our thoughts are influenced by emotions before we can even think them often! It also dates back to remembering how someone or matter made you feel as the emotional memory space is stored for you to mentally think about down the road.

- Emotionally: This seems like an obvious one however the emotional component of emotions is usually oddly the hardest part for most people to grasp! It exists within us beyond the physical and mental elements somewhere. This is the primary of emotion itself; what we feel, how we experience, and the role these feelings play inside our lives. Simply, it is the overall emotional condition of being.

Feelings create an endless response cycle between your physical body and brain for better or worse. They can control your activities or help enhance them - this all depends on your personal relationship with them and your emotional state to be. Overall, feelings are responses to different circumstances that go far beyond the physical features of chemicals releasing within the body.

Emotional senses range between cheerfulness, shock, and anxiety, to sorrow, hatred, and rage. Although feelings are an important part of human living, they may affect your personal conduct and sometimes, you can risk attaching feelings to everything.

Although these skills are essential for the workplace, they will help you improve your relationships outside of work also. To build up, and perfect, your emotional intelligence you need to start paying even more attention to emotions, yours' and others', start to pay attention more and talk less, and make an effort to become more available to other people's viewpoint.

4 tips about how to develop emotional intelligence:

<u>Get to know yourself</u>

Try to realize why you feel a certain way, and what had triggered such feelings. When the triggers are known by you, you can either prevent certain situations or, if they're unavoidable, find a real way of dealing with them. Understanding triggers help deepen your self-consciousness because this can help you learn how certain situations, emotions or people cause you to feel, and why. It is rather important you learn to never ignore your emotions, even negative ones, but to identify them and cope with them.

<u>Try to understand others</u>

Unfortunately, most of us are often too busy to treatment. Life has become extremely complicated and competitive, because of which, just maintaining your head above water is normally a challenge, aside from sharing what small spare energy or time you have with others.

Besides, in the Western culture, along with in societies where there is a high turnover of people and staff constantly maneuver around, changing jobs and cities they live in regularly, most of the associations are superficial and based on interest. To understand someone else's motives and feelings, you need to be willing to devote your undivided mind and attention to that person. You have to really want to understand their behavior and attitude, to listen attentively all night if you have to, to be content for them, or become sad with them.

This is often particularly hard in case you are working with someone who is filled with long-held anger or frustration. So, although empathy can be developed with perseverance and great listening skills, those people who are naturally caring and compassionate will be the most empathetic.

Think that before you speak

Once you identify your emotion and know what had triggered it, take some time to comprehend it and "procedure" it, before responding to it. Basically, allow it sink in before you react. If overwhelmed with emotions, it may help to ask yourself why you feel the true way you do. When you know why something had produced you feel angry, betrayed or embarrassed, it becomes much easier deciding what the next step should be.

Learn about the importance of self-management

If you figure out how to identify, control, and express your emotions, you should understand how to use them in ways that's most effective under the situations. Many people underestimate the importance of expressing their feelings in an adult way. Like ignoring or repressing emotions is bad for your health just, so is overreacting, ie expressing emotions without the consideration for how they may affect others.

Therefore, continue reminding yourself that although held-back emotions create tension, both and externally internally, those expressed in a rush and without thinking are like shooting without aiming. The ultimate way to improve your self-management is to have significantly more psychological self-control and constantly work on enhancing your integrity.

some techniques of emotional intelligence used for manipulation

<u>Develop self-awareness</u>

Self-awareness is about self-knowledge, about getting mindful of what is happening in your life, and about having an idea how you see your daily life or career developing. To be self-aware you need a certain degree of maturity and at least a vague idea of what you'd like to do with your existence. When you know what you want, it becomes easier to find a method of getting it. If you don't, you are left drifting aimlessly, with neither a goal nor a plan.

So, how can you develop self-awareness? Begin by increasing your sensitivity to your very own gut and emotions emotions, as they are generally the most trusted close friends you'll ever have. Make an effort to set aside a while for self-reflection, and think about your behavior, thoughts, emotions, frustrations, goals, etc.

Those who are used to self-analysis will find this easy probably, but if you're not used to this type or sort of thinking, this may be hard, even unsettling. In that full case, start by setting aside 30 minutes each night, once you're finished with the work for the day and may relax a bit, and think about the day or week behind you. If you had a difficult day/week particularly, ask yourself everything you can find out from the experience.

The purpose of this exercise is to truly get you used to considering how you feel and why.

Or, you may start journaling, and this is not about keeping a diary and covering your day-to-day thoughts and activities. Journaling is about recording any unusual or frustrating experiences, thoughts or emotions you might have had. Some things are not easy to go over with others, and anyway, not really everything is for posting, so why not get it off your chest by authoring it. The great thing about journaling is normally that to write something down, you need to believe about what to write, in fact it is often this technique of thinking about a problem that helps you see what's at the root of it. Therefore, if feeling upset, angry or disappointed, write it out and move on.

Understand your emotions and what triggers them

To comprehend your emotions you have to be willing to experience them. It's sad just how many people are afraid of their own emotions, especially negative ones, eg sadness, anger, bitterness, etc and the moment they feel these feelings taking over, they perform something that may interrupt their train of thought, eg they could active themselves with something in order to distract themselves from these unpleasant emotions.

In the event that you recognize yourself in this, you should know that all you will achieve this way is postpone (perhaps indefinitely) facing your own demons and dealing with whatever it is that's troubling you. Feelings need to be experienced and dealt with, not buried.

Intelligent folks are not scared of their emotions emotionally. Whatever it really is they feel, they keep at it for so long as it requires for the emotion to end up being identified. There is a reason you feel how you do, and instead of ignoring them, you should try to "decipher" your emotions because they are trying to let you know something.

To become proficient at understanding others, you first have to be able to understand yourself. So, even the emotions you don't actually want to feel should be addressed, processed, and let go.

Listen without judging

Good listeners are uncommon, mainly because this involves a whole lot of empathy, willingness to give up your time and effort for others, and mental energy to be present when you are listening.

The primary trait of a good listener is to pay attention with empathy, and which means without judging. This is not easy always, and may in a few full cases be difficult, so if you understand you are biased towards someone, it's perhaps better not to talk to them in the event that you know you have already made up your mind about how you are feeling about what they are going to say.

So, to become a great listener you should attempt to be present during the conversation, and stay focused. This can be hard, as some social people don't stop talking, or have a problem stating what they mean so you may be looking at a few hours. However, if you are not interested in this person really, or you are in a rush, or are not feeling well, try to postpone the conversation for another time. The tell-tale indications of disinterest or boredom, eg glancing at your watch, or checking your cell emails or phone, can be extremely insulting and discouraging for the person you are having a conversation with.

Emotionally intelligent people show interest in others by encouraging them to speak even more (even if indeed they don't agree with what they are saying), and by creating a host where it's safe to start and say everything you really mean.

So, the next time you speak to a person who requirements your opinion, advice or simply a shoulder to cry on, try to be patient (some people have a long time to come to the point), focused (reserve this time limited to them and switch off your phone), and non-judgemental (provide them with the benefit of a doubt). By not becoming and judging open-minded, you might not only help the person by giving them an opportunity to obtain something off their upper body, nevertheless, you may also gain insight into what's going on in your team, or a family.

Also, focus on body language, both yours' and theirs', eg the modulation of voice, facial expression, body posture, etc. To a casual observer, these would be clear symptoms how you both feel about the conversation.

Active listening takes a complete lot of practice, but it is among those skills that you can practice every full day, of where you are regardless, and what it really is you are listening to.

Mind-Body Connection

This is about listening to the body and understanding what it's trying to tell you. According to the mind-body connection doctrine, irritation in a part of your body is definitely a sure indication something is not right. For instance, lower back discomfort is linked to financial problems, upper back discomfort to being overwhelmed with life, a knot in the tummy with nervousness or fear, etc.

Understanding how to notice these signals and interpret them, can help you save considerable time and difficulty with regards to understanding why you feel a certain way.

But, what frequently happens is that while your body is informing you that you are anxious, anxious, angry, or harm, you ignore these symptoms simply, hoping they would eventually go away.

Unfortunately, Western culture pays an excessive amount of importance to feeling happy and high at all times, so folks are not encouraged to deal with their negative feelings, but are advised to ignore them, eg by repeating positive affirmations, or repair them, by taking something that will make them experience better. Do you really believe that if you ignore your adverse feelings, do it again a mantra or take something to make you feel high, you will eventually become happy, confident, and fearless???

Sometimes, when you're overwhelmed with emotions, it may be OK to calm yourself straight down, in unhealthy ways even, until you may clearly think. But, this only gives temporary respite and is not a solution to your problem.

Emotional intelligence will help you get to underneath of your emotions by showing you how exactly to work out what the triggers are, and how exactly to interpret and release these emotions in the least harmful way.

<u>Engage</u>

How involved are you with your community? Do you volunteer? Is there someone you are helping with by moral support frequently, financially or otherwise? Are you there for others if they need you even though you know it'll ruin your weekend which you had planned to invest with your family?

Empathy is the primary trait of intelligent people emotionally, and it could easily be developed by anyone if they follow a couple of simple tips on how to develop or improve these abilities. But, the simplest way to develop empathy can be through practicing it. Put simply, whenever you engage with others, you are doing what emotionally smart people do: you listen, you try to understand, you listen in.

Nevertheless, many people fake empathy due to the fact they'd like to be observed simply because emotionally intelligent. They say the right matter, are politically correct always, appear to be filled with deep empathy, listen thoroughly, offer help, etc. However, if caught off-safeguard or if for a few good reason not feeling in the feeling for putting up an act, their true character quickly comes out. Today, to advance professionally, if you see yourself as a head especially, you have to prove that you have high psychological intelligence, so those that fake it do that for self-promotion usually.

The easiest way to improve your empathy is to start taking interest in others, eg how they live, what's troubling them, how they cope, etc. Improve your listening skills and try to possess at least one deep conversation per month. By engaging with others, you automatically increase your emotional intelligence.

Develop self-management

Self-management is about controlling your emotions, not in the feeling that you suppress them or ignore them, but figure out how to deal with them, and only release them after you have processed and understood them. Self-management is also about being accurate to yourself. Some of the real ways you can improve your self-administration are through developing your integrity, eg:

- Practice what you preach

- Be prepared to speak up, even though you risk being made fun of

- Don't make promises you are unlikely to keep

- Continually be polite and respectful with co-workers, it doesn't matter how close you might be

- Be self-disciplined, especially if you anticipate that of others

<u>Learn to cope with criticism</u>

Negative feedback is usually often undeserved and a result of the person presenting it is not fully aware of your performance, or using the opportunity to sabotage your self-confidence perhaps, or undermine your job openly.

However, if truth be told, atlanta divorce attorneys negative feedback there is usually a grain of truth. Although there might have been very good reasons why you underperformed or experienced a score of people complain about you, the truth is you failed. However, when you come to a stage when you're able to accept negative opinions, or open criticism, without taking it you demonstrate which you have both self-confidence and psychological intelligence personally.

So, how to become more open to negative feedback? Of all first, not all criticism is important equally, nor should you react to it in the same way. A colleague's remark about your brand-new hairstyle is actually a sign she's making fun of you, nonetheless it may be a subtle suggestion that the design doesn't suit you.

Besides, in the event that you receive less than satisfactory feedback on your own performance repeatedly, or behavior, instead of sulking or throwing a tantrum, try to look in yourself through other people's eye. Imagine if you ARE lazy actually, or short-tempered, or unreliable?

The key thing is to consider why you are feeling bad about the feedback. Is it because it's really undeserved and due to the person giving it devoid of a complete picture, or are you angry with yourself for not having masked your underperformance better? Or simply jealous others do better?

Admitting you were wrong isn't easy, but surviving in denial is even worse. So, than experience upset about the opinions rather, try to find out something from it. Especially if it's not the very first time the same thing have been brought to your attention.

But, regardless of how you feel, be aware that negative feedback, if given without malice, can perform more for your personal development, than can false praise.

Besides, there is something noble about admitting you had been wrong. It could not be a pleasant thing to do, but it teaches you are mature more than enough to take both the credit for your successes and blamc for your errors. This may encourage others to do the same.

Chapter 5: Body Language and Manipulation

Some people are naturals at reading others, but they couldn't tell you how they know what they know. That's because they are intuitively reading others' body language, but they don't have the knowledge to define why they are such good communicators. More than 70 percent of the messages we send and receive are through non-verbal language. Not only are the greatest percent of our messages non-verbal, but that non-verbal language is more honest and genuine than the words we speak. Our bodies don't sugar coat the message; we just respond and react without being conscious of doing so.

If people are saying one thing but their body language is delivering a different message, put more stock in what you see than what you hear. However, to make sure you are reading the person correctly, let's discuss all the different nonverbal messages we send. We'll cover the nonverbal signals and what they might mean, but keep in mind that different cultures and countries might attach a different meaning to your body language. When you're confused about the nonverbal message that another is sending, then listen to the words and take the signals in context with the phrases they use.

Another way to determine the message is through the tone, pitch, and volume of another's voice. It gives truth to that saying, "It's not what you said but how you said it." When all these things are examined during your analysis of others, you'll find clarity in the message. While we're at it, there is one more thing—pay attention to the other person's required personal space. If you are questioning whether the message they are sending is positive, negative, or benevolent, step inside their personal space and be aware of their reaction. Their feelings will then be quite pronounced. If the message was meant to be off-putting, they will immediately step back or adopt a space-claiming stance that will let you know their feelings in no uncertain terms.

Facial Expressions, Features, and Head Movement

• Playing with Hair and Moving the Head

If someone slides their fingers through their hair at the temples and tosses their head back, this is an indication they might be flirting with you. On the other hand, if they are running their fingers through their hair from their forehead through the top of their crown, that is a sign they are confused or frustrated. Tilting the head and twirling the hair is also a flirtatious mannerism, indicating interest combined with a little nervous tension.

When people nod their heads, it matters how many times they do so before stopping. For example, public speakers who are attentive to their audiences know that three nods mean interest and attentiveness. However, if you observe a group of people conversing, you'll notice the person who nods their head only once is eager to leave and will probably be the next one to make a quick exit.

If someone is interested in what you're saying, they will often tilt their head in your direction. They could be showing curiosity or questioning what you are saying when they bring one ear closer to make sure they are getting every detail of the conversation.

• Eye Movement

People usually blink six or seven times a minute, but those who are stressed blink quite a bit more. If someone covers their eyes with their hands, excessively rubs their eyes, or closes their eyes, they could be hiding something or feel threatened. When the eyes are shifty or rapidly moving from one person to another, it reflects some scattered thoughts that are going on in their heads. If there is a flickering interest between two people when this is happening, then it can also be a way for people to prevent detection as they were checking out the other.

If someone has a habit of not making eye contact or looking down as they speak, it can show shyness or can also be a cry for empathy. They are waiting for you to ask what's wrong and open the way for them to share their feelings. Investigators have come to realize that a sustained glance from a person who denies involvement in a crime, may mean they are lying and trying to over-compensate by looking them straight in the eyes for a long time to show they're telling the truth.

If you have posed a question and the person you asked looks upward, they are most likely trying to picture something they saw. On the other hand, if they look to the side toward their ear, they could be trying to recall a message they heard. If they look downward after your question, they are connecting your question with something negative and trying to find a way to avoid answering or revealing their feelings about the matter.

- Eyebrow Movement

If individuals raise their eyebrows, it usually means the person is curious about or interested in your conversation. A quick popup of one eyebrow could be a flirtation, and if the eyebrow is raised a bit longer, it often means that the other person doesn't quite buy into what you say.

If the brows furrow, you can almost bet that person is having second thoughts about what is being done or said. It most likely indicates a negative emotion like fear or confusion, so it might be time for you to back off a bit.

- ● Lips

Of course, a smile sends a universal message, if it is truly a smile. We've all been at the other end of a fake smile, which is one that doesn't travel all the way to the eyes and make them wrinkle in agreement. We call those "Red Carpet" smiles. They are Hollywood smiles given by people who are trying to be friendly to their fans but just want to get inside, sit down, and make it through the night.

Individuals who plaster a smile on their face almost all the time, are usually nervous. If it's in the workplace, they could feel out-of-their-depth or incompetent. There's a good chance that foreigners who smile a lot don't understand a blasted thing, so they just smile and nod.

Another thing people do with their lips is to suck on them and bite them. Sucking or biting the lip is a reaction by those who need to settle themselves down. Like a newborn, the action soothes them and offers a bit of comfort in a stressful situation. If one clamps down on their lips or purses them, it can mean frustration or anger.

Body and Limb Movements

- ● Body Positions

If there is a group of people standing and talking and one or more people open their bodies to you, that is an invitation to join the conversation. If they just turn their head, you might want to choose another group. You will know if you have captured the attentions of a love interest because he or she will turn slightly toward you and point their feet in your direction, to indicate they are interested in finding out what makes you tick. If you step into the group and the person beside you touches your shoulder or arm, this is a direct ploy to show you they are interested in exploring the relationship a bit further.

When you step into the group, if the person beside you leans into you, they genuinely like you. If their head retracts backward, perhaps something you said surprised or offended them. If they physically lean away from you, they've already made up their mind that they're not going to listen to or like you. If they turn their head in the opposite direction and follow it with their shoulder, you just got the cold shoulder. So, forget about it!

• Standing Positions

If someone is standing with legs about shoulder width apart, it often is a sign of dominance and determination, as if they needed to stand their ground against something or prove a point. If they stand with legs together, front forward, they will hear you out, but you need to make your point quickly. When the person you are speaking with is standing and shifting their weight from side-to-side or front-to-back, it might indicate several things. They could be bored, or they are anxious and need to sooth themselves with this rocking sort of movement. To determine their feelings, it is necessary to look further at what they are doing with their arms as well.

- **Arm Positions**

Don't assume that crossed arms always mean that the other person is upset. Not so! Some people will stand or sit with their arms crossed because it is just a comfortable position. You can distinguish the other's emotions by looking further at their facial expression. If they have furrowed eyebrows, their mouth pursed, and their arms crossed, chances are they are angry or upset about something. Crossed arms can also be a sign of protection or a closed attitude to the ideas you are presenting.

If someone is talking with their arms flopping around, it can mean they are excited and agreeable, or it can say that they are out of control. Again, you'll need to couple your observations with other nonverbal messages to be sure. Typically, people who are overly animated are less believable and have less control over their emotions, as well as having a lack of power. They flail their arms to gain attention as if to say "I'm talking now, so would somebody please listen to me?"

- ## Leg and Foot Positions

People whose toes turn inward could be closing themselves off to your comments, or they could just be pigeon-toed. To determine if there is a physiological issue that causes their toes to point it, you might need more background information. Don't rush to judgment, just wait, observe more body language, and listen to their words. Some people who began turning in their toes because they were insecure or awkward, might have created a habit that they find difficult to break. The only message they are sending is one that says; I have a physical issue that is impacting my body language.

- ## Sitting Positions

If a person is spread out all over your couch, they have a feeling of self-importance. On the other hand, they probably have a good deal of confidence as well. Legs open, leaning forward with elbows on knees shows an in-charge attitude that is still open to hearing what you have to say.

If a person is sitting next to you and crosses their legs at the knee, pointing their foot toward you, they are giving you permission to approach them. If, however, they are sitting next to you and angle their body in the opposite direction, you're probably not going to engage or connect with him or her. If that same person is fidgeting, quickly moving their ankle or foot, they are looking for a way out. Excuse yourself; both of you will probably feel more comfortable.

• Hands

When people sit on their hands, and the temperatures aren't below freezing, it could be an indication that they are deceitful—trying to hide something from you. If they walk with their hands in their pockets or behind their back, they might be relaying information, but you're not getting the full picture because they are withholding information. When you look at one's fingers and see bitten nails or chewed cuticles, you can bet that is a nervous person with low self-esteem. Or else they have put themselves in a situation that they find extremely uncomfortable.

When someone holds their hands like a church steeple and presses them to their lips, they have something important to add to the conversation but are trying to decide how to present their information. They are self-assured and will contribute when the time is right. These are the thinkers, the analytical types.

If the person is rubbing their legs with open palms pressed down, they are feeling vulnerable or uncomfortable with your nearness or your conversation. If nothing is said, don't think you are not sending a message that is perhaps louder than any words. Examine your body language and see what message you are sending to them that could be creating this reaction.

• Walking

People who advance with rather large strides are purposeful and perceived as important and competent. People think those who walk with a little bounce in their step most likely have a positive nature. And those who walk hunched over with shoulders down—well, that kind of speaks for itself, doesn't it? They are probably prone to depression and wrapped a bit too tight.

What Does One's Voice Say About Them?

There are four indicators of the quality of one's voice. They are one's intonation, volume, pitch, and rate of speech. If the voice is monotone and rather flat, they are probably bored or boring. The lack of animation in the voice could also indicate the speaker is tired. If the person's voice sounds clear and concise, they most usually are confident and powerful, more like the Leader Personality Type. If the volume is quiet or soft, the person is thought to be shy, or it could even mean they have a secret they don't want to share.

The rate of speech is also quite important when analyzing others, especially if you are attempting to mirror them to increase the chances of connectivity. For example, Leader Personality Types will usually speak fast and loud, and you need to match their volume and rate. Identifiers often speak slower than Leaders, and their pitch is more soothing than the dominant personality type. The voice can be a strong descriptive element of the individual's personality type.

By now, you have probably caught on that every movement has a message. Verify the meaning of some of the nonverbal languages by other things, such as one's words, voice, facial expressions, and gestures. To discover one's real message, you must become a student of human behavior, studying the other's movements, speech pattern, attitude, words, gestures, and expressions to analyze people successfully.

You've been introduced to the nonverbal language and the four main personality types, and to how you form accurate perceptions, but all these things are not separate from one another. They all blend to create effective communications. In the next chapter, you'll be asked to read some scenarios and identify the personality types, nonverbal indicators, and interpret the intended message.

some techniques of body language used for manipulation

You've already learned how to analyze nonverbal language, but the key to excellent communications is knowing how to interpret and respond to the messages others send so that you can connect with them on a much more effective level. Wouldn't it be wonderful not to wonder what a person is thinking? Instead of questioning whether people are agreeable or accepting of your suggestions or opinions, you can use all the strategies you have learned in this book to look beyond the spoken word and read the hidden feelings people might be entertaining.

Some personality types are naturally more suited to one another, while others trigger feelings of annoyance and impatience, depending upon their key traits and character preferences. By examining each personality type a bit further, you'll gain some insight into why you instantly hit it off with some people and others just rub you the wrong way.

Leaders with Other Leaders

Partnering two Leader Personality Types is like putting two alpha dogs together in the same arena. Each one fights to lead, with nobody left to follow through and complete the task. With such competitive natures, Leaders struggle with one another to manipulate and control their environment. They are both sure their strategies and methodologies are the best, and compromise is not one of their strengths. For these reasons, placing two Leaders on a project can create unnecessary power plays, unless one's secondary personality type is a Fraternizer or Identifier.

When the relationship is personal, a coupling of two Leaders can be all work and no fun. If each is career-minded individuals, your lives will most likely not revolve around each other, but be centered on work-related events and projects. It is common when two career professionals hook up, for a while they will be quite intrigued by one another's focus and business acumen. However, as the relationship matures, the Leaders will tend to be more attentive to work-related issues, and their personal relationships suffer. If you are a Leader involved with another Leader Personality Type, you'll need to challenge one another on a personal level to keep the fires burning. Compete in a mutually enjoyed sport, or find a thrill-seeking, competitive hobby that interest both of you. It's necessary to be involved in one another's home life as well as your business endeavors.

Leaders with Perceivers

Leaders usually work well with Perceiver Personality Types because they are organizers and analytical thinkers, and their quiet, unemotional demeanor typically satisfies the Leader's goal-driven manner. The Perceiver doesn't challenge the Leader for "top dog" position because he or she doesn't enjoy being the center of attention. The downside to partnering a Leader with a Perceiver is that the professional or personal relationship can be cold and rather unexciting unless there are some Fraternizer traits in one or the other's personality.

Leaders with Fraternizers or Identifiers

If the Fraternizers or Identifiers have some secondary Perceiver or Leader traits, they will do well when relating to people who are almost all Leader types. However, if the Fraternizer or Identifier is strong in their personality traits, their empathetic and emotional behaviors will often grate on the Leader's last nerve. What Fraternizers and Identifiers need to do when communicating with a Leader or Perceiver Types is to learn to curb their feelings and reign in their emotions when interacting with these strong personalities.

The two personality types that are usually not good to put together are Leader to Leader and Fraternizer to Fraternizer, and here's why. As we said before, two Leaders will fight for the controlling position. Examining the Fraternizers, they too are competitive, and they will experience a struggle unique to their type. Fraternizers will almost always try to one-up each other, challenging one another to a more dangerous sport or a project that requires greater and greater risks. Or, Fraternizers will turn everything into such fun that there will be no work accomplished. So, let's examine how to respond best to each personality type.

Communicating with an Identifier

Avoid getting too emotional when talking with an Identifier Personality Type. Since they are rather indecisive, you'll need to continually pull them back to the task at hand and discuss the decision to make and its' probably outcome. Identifiers enjoy talking about feelings, and they will be sensitive to yours. While this is good in a personal relationship, in the office it can be distracting.

If the Identifier is your direct report, their open-door policy will enable others to frequently interrupt your time with them, creating difficulties when trying to get them to stay on task. So, be patient; your frustration will not change their policies; it will only serve to make you look grumpy and cynical. After their interruptions, they'll be tempted to discuss the other person's problems with you, which will take you further down the rabbit hole. So, count on your meetings with Identifiers taking longer and achieving less.

There is almost always delays in projects as well. The Identifier will want you to check with other team members to see how they feel about any new ideas or changes, no matter how seemingly insignificant. Or, they will insist on discussing this issue in another meeting with more managers and team members. If you aren't careful, beginning a project can take a month of meetings.

In your personal relationships, Identifiers can be a bit moody and overly sensitive. If you are a Leader personality involved with a significant other who is an Identifier, you need to get comfortable with a relationship that is emotionally demanding. Also, your need to stay focused and move forward may make them feel as though they are not being heard or valued. As a Leader, you will need to slow down and allow the Identifier to fulfill his or her need to nurture and comfort. You won't be allowed to hide away when you're sick, and too many evenings spent working at the office is going to create some emotional outbursts.

Communicating with a Perceiver

Being in a personal relationship with a Perceiver Personality Type can be a guessing game. They don't like to share their feelings, and they can be a bit stand-offish, so if you are an Identifier that needs more reassurance, just know that you're not going to get it from the Perceiver. They might have deep feelings for you, but sharing those feelings is a challenge for them.

On the other hand, if you show too many emotions in the relationship, they'll be confused and draw further back into their comfortable, quiet shell of self-protection. Perceivers can also be rather stubborn and set in their ways, so getting them to change is like pulling teeth. If you do expect change, make sure you give them plenty of time to think things through and avoid popping any surprises on them, no matter how pleasant you think it will be for them to experience the change.

For example, Laurie decided it would be a great birthday present to replace her husband, Al's football chair. It was embarrassingly worn, and the springs were giving way, so she felt he would be much more comfortable watching his favorite programs in a nice, cushy, new recliner. As a surprise, Laurie had the new chair delivered while Al was at work, and they took the tattered one away. She didn't quite get the reaction she was hoping for when Al returned from work. Although he has never complained much about his old chair, Al has merely changed his favorite seating area to a corner of the couch.

Al might have liked the idea of having a new chair had Laurie not surprised him with the idea and had his old one hauled away before he was ready for the change. He needed time to adjust to the idea that another chair could be just as comfortable, and he could have gone to the store, sat in a gazillion chairs, then slowly made his mind up to purchase the first one in which he plopped. However, without having the opportunity to think it over, look at the chairs to decide which one best suited him, and then compare prices and warranties, Al was not thrilled with Laurie's birthday present.

Communicating with a Fraternizer

Fraternizer Personality Types can get along with almost anyone, but some personality types will eventually grow weary of their tired jokes and constant need for entertainment. Also, a Perceiver will not appreciate the spontaneous spending that many Fraternizers practice. A died-in-the-wool Fraternizer with few secondary personality traits that are more grounded is often too immature and impulsive for a Leader of Perceiver in their personal relationships.

In the workplace, Fraternizers are often perceived as party people and not taken seriously. No matter how intelligent, many Fraternizers are not promoted to their potential because they allow their fun-loving spirit too much free reign in the workplace. Fraternizers usually don't make good quarterly budget planners because they spend too freely and are too rash when it comes to decision-making. If you work with a Fraternizer, you will need to keep them focused and grounded to achieve success with projects in which you are both involved.

Examining Some Personal Scenarios

Think of a co-working with whom you are currently experiencing some challenges when communicating with him or her. Now review the following questions to determine the other person's personality type and what you can do to create a more positive working relationship.

- What is your subject's dominant personality type? How do you know this?

- What is your dominant personality type?

- What does this person do that annoys you? Analyze these behaviors to see if this is a trait of their personality type?

- What do you think you are doing that annoys him or her?

- Is this your imagination, or are you reading their non-verbal language?

- What was the last challenge you experienced with him or her?

- Based on his or her personality type, how could you have responded better to create a more positive outcome?

- Knowing what you know now, how will you communicate with this person in the future to create a better relationship?

Now, think of a personal relationship you would like to improve and ask yourself the same questions. When you determine the other's personality type, make sure you verify your beliefs by observing their behaviors, listening to their words, and analyzing the body language they are displaying around you. Ask yourself if you are too sensitive because of your personality type, or if you really are having serious communication issues with this person.

Scientifically Proven Methods of Non-Verbal Influence

We've discussed the need to read other people's attitudes and perspectives by observing their body language, as part of your influential arsenal. In any case, communication is a two-way interaction. You're also being "read" by those you interact with. Even if people don't boast the same level of awareness of non-verbal communication you do, they are still registering what you're saying without words. This is why it's so important that you master this aspect of communication in order to use it effectively. The perceptions of others are being shaped in every move you make, quite literally. This is true, even if that perception is subconscious. That subconscious impression can impact the willingness of others to work with and cooperate with you, so learning to send the right message is crucial.

Let's take a look at some aspects of body language and what they say to others, taking note of any habits you may model which need remediation:

Dilated Pupils

As Psychologist Eckhard Hess established in 1975, your pupils dilate when you are highly interested in what the person talking is saying. When you notice the dilation of someone's pupils, you're in a good position to move further toward your goal of influencing that person to take your part in whatever goal it is you have in mind. Strike while the iron is hot. This applies to all spheres of your life - social, business life and family.

Body Position

Being aware of how you're positioned in relation to those you're addressing is a fundamental skill. Are you facing them directly? Then it's important that other aspects of your body language don't indicate aggression, as facing someone directly can have that effect, if your hands are on your hips, your head is thrown back with your chin up, or you're standing too close to the other person. Placing your hands in front of you, with your fingers laced, is a non-confrontational way of saying you're not a threatening person. Placing your hands behind your back is another way, but may also be interpreted as submission, particularly if your feet are close together. With feet wider apart, this arm and hand position is much more effective and signals openness.

Turning away from someone may indicate that you're attempting to avoid a confrontation, or that you're not truly engaged in the conversation. In can also mean you don't trust or like the person in question. Again, the position of the arms and hands is key to understanding the message. Folding one arm across your chest to hold the arm closest the other party (as though half-hugging yourself), indicates shyness, as does wrapping both arms around the body in a self-hugging motion.

Following your gaze

Someone who follows your gaze wherever you divert it, is likely to be a progressive thinker. Conservative thinkers will not do this. The gaze will remain fixed and static. Following the gaze is also an indication of mirroring, practiced either consciously or unconsciously. As we've discussed elsewhere, mirroring is a sign of familiarity and common cause, which generally means that we're reaching out to the other party without words.

Physical/Verbal Dissonance

The person you are speaking to may present a calm and unruffled façade (or at least be endeavoring to do that. You may, at first glance, believe this person to be attentive to what you're saying, but there are signs that break through the façade. Being attentive to these can be helpful in determining whether the person you're talking to is either zoning out or is preoccupied.

Crossing and uncrossing the legs, when seated, is one such indication. Restless hands are another, including constant movement of the hands, adjusting clothing, picking at the fingernails, rubbing the fingers and lacing and unlacing the fingers. People who are not engaging with you, but who prefer to pretend that this is the case, instead of indicating an interest in ending the conversation, are either being unduly polite, or deliberately deceptive. The eyes can determine which of these is true.

Continual blinking is a strong signal that the person you're talking to is unwilling·to continue the conversation, but even more unwilling to own up to their discomfort, boredom or need to move on to something else, as the time they've allotted to the discussion has elapsed.

Stand with shoulders square

If you want the trust and support of others, you need to display resolute confidence. Maintaining a confident bearing involves good posture and squaring the shoulders while in conversation. When accompanied by similarly squaring your feet, this may seem confrontational, but can be very useful in establishing primacy in difficult situations. Body language like this is reasonably aggressive, but can be modified by placing the hands behind the back, or amplified by placing the hands on the hips (ultra-aggressive, as discussed earlier.

Of primary importance is good posture, which sends a strong message of confidence and self-awareness.

<u>Leaning in</u>

If you lean towards the person you're engaging, chances are that person is going to stop speaking and listen to what you have to say. This works, whether you are standing or seated. This posture tends to make you appear dominant. The other person will read leaning in to mean that you are serious about what you are saying and that you expect to be heard.

As you can see, your body language can influence other people by more intensely focusing your message; complementing your words with supportive physical cues. Being attentive to maintaining body language which correlates with your spoken message will not only make you more effective in your interactions with others, but signals your personal integrity. That's powerful.

Chapter 6: Manipulation Skills to Gain Friends

Is it always easy to make friends in a new environment? Of course not! Sometimes it is extremely intimidating and at other times, downright hostile. Other times, you feel like fish out of water. Everybody needs friends and learning how to attract them is an important life skill we should all have. Human beings are fundamentally social animals who seek out the company of others and there are very few exceptions to that rule.

Choosing friends – Drawing the kind of friends you'd like to have

Here are three broad categories of friends:

Hello-Bye-bye friends (acquaintances)

These are people who become your friends almost automatically, by virtue of finding yourselves in the same environment, like your workplace, for example. You say "hello" when you meet the first time in the day and you say "bye-bye" as you wind up for the day. Once away from the shared environment, these friends (which are actually only acquaintances) rarely have any further involvement with you. They're nice to know and they can be valuable allies, due to their skills, but they're not necessarily the sort of people you can count on one hand. (The Greeks say that you can count true friends on one hand – that's something to keep in mind).

The Average Buddy

Drinking buddies, golf buddies, shopping pals – fun time friends come and go. They share with you the things about life that make it fun, because they're fun. They like to laugh and enjoy your company. The lighter side of life is where these friends are going to pop up. These aren't necessarily people you engage in long conversations about the meaning of life, or the reality of climate change. This is your loose social circle, developed over time, that enjoys a good time as much as you do. They come and go and when you meet, a good time is had by all, but there's little in the way of depth in the relationship.

Soul friends

These are the 3:00 am phone call friends. You know they'll be ready to talk if you wake them from a sound sleep. These are the people you can go on a road trip with and not want to kill before you've even hit Route 66.

Long, probing conversations, shared secrets and mutual support are what these friends are all about. People who stick with you, through thick and thin, are soul friends. They're the people who have an intimate understanding of what makes you tick and you return the favor. Some of these friends may be with you from childhood until death. Others, you may pick up along the way. What distinguishes them from the hello bye-byes and average buddies is the depth of the relationship. You may go years without seeing a soul friend, but when you finally meet up again, it's as though no time has passed. You pick up where you left off, because you know each other so well and you were meant to be friends. These are the ones who are the hardest to find and also the ones you long for. Soul friends are a reflection of who we are and what we really care about. Even more than that, they're the people we know we can always count on, because they know exactly who we are.

Forming genuine friendships takes time

True friends are not made overnight. True, lasting and intimate friendships evolve over time, due to a genuine chemistry that exists between the people involved. Like romantic relationships, friendships are based in a fundamental chemical exchange which speaks to both parties like a song. You know when it's real. You can't create these bonds. They're pre-existing realities that you can only recognize and act on. When true friends; soul friends come into your life, the impact will be unforgettable. You will know immediately that the person you've just met is intended to be with you (in whatever capacity) until the end of your life. Soul friends may not always be at our side, physically, but they will always be at our side, spiritually. Where ever we are and whatever we're doing, we know they're there. We know we can pick up the phone, call and find them ready to talk to us. These are the friends who are with us until we're no longer living and breathing. That's what makes them so special and so incredibly important.

While we may recognize a soul friend at first sight, the world is not a place in which bonds are easily formed on this level. Soul friends, despite the distrust we've all learned to live with in the modern world, will look beyond that initial reticence and continue showing up. They won't give up. They'll seek you out, even when they don't know they're doing it and you'll do the same. Over time, the bond will become unbreakable and you will have made a friend for life.

Here is how you can become adept at making new friends:

Don't over think

Have you been apprehensive about meeting someone only for you to feel at home with them in the first two minutes of meeting? The fact is that if you are meeting a person for the first time, you have no idea how they are or how they behave. Why bother analyzing everything half to death?

And again, assuming that meeting with a new person is bound to be scary only serves to make you fearful of the moment. The fear then makes you wary of the meeting; sometimes even making you detest it. In fact, for the most part, the reason you find yourself feeling somewhat shy towards a person is because of the fear you are harboring of having an encounter with them, or anyone else for that matter. Life makes us into individual silos of isolation. It makes us suspicious. Bad experiences with other people can stunt our ability to form the kind of bonds we're actually hungry for – the kind of bonds that last a life time. The best solution, therefore, is to disabuse yourself of the notion that meeting people you are not familiar with is scary. Stop over-thinking about how to carry out that first conversation; how to connect with people who are actually the kind of people you need in your life. Overthinking the forging of the most important connections in our lives can make of us sad, isolated people who never really connect with others in the profound and lasting way that human beings were intended to connect.

After all, who is to tell if the other party is not anxious about meeting you? We're all anxious in these latter days. We're all suspicious and nervous and continually asking ourselves if the people we meet have the right motivations; if they're genuine. Most of us are thinking the same thing. We've lost our trust in one another.

So relax and create in your mind a positive image of that first encounter; a healthy image. In any case, there are plenty of people out there who may judge you unfairly on your first encounter. Everyone carries around a collection of cultural assumptions about the composition of people who are worth knowing. You have them too. The trick is to open yourself to others and to allow the universe to connect you. It works very well, if you'll allow it to happen. People worth having as friends know better than to judge a person on superficial grounds. In summary, fear is in your mind – get rid of it! Let go of your accumulated fears and presuppositions and, instead, rely on your intuitive powers and your newly-established ability to read people. You know enough to understand when people are honest or not. You've learned to read their mannerisms, their speech patterns, their facial expressions and other non-verbal indicators about who they are. Trust yourself and your knowledge. You're more than ready to sift the wheat from the chaff, which means there's absolutely nothing to fear; no cause for suspicion or reticence.

You're now more than ready to throw yourself out into the social whirl and find the kind of people who deserve to have as friends. With your new skills, rooted in the practice of social psychology, you're going to be able to establish rather quickly who is naughty and who is nice. The Big Bad Wolf is out there, but you're not Little Red Riding Hood anymore. You're now a proficient and capable, socially aware person. No one's pulling the wool over your eyes anymore. With your new knowledge, it will be easy for you to discern, from the people you meet, who is going to be the kind of friend you need in your life. There's no more guesswork, because you know the ropes now.

Move at your own pace

If you have been out of the social scene for a while, you may feel overwhelmed meeting new people, as you ease yourself back into it (say in a seminar or even a party). However, you can pre-empt that problem by seeking out individual friends or acquaintances who you expect to be in attendance. You can meet with them before the event and catch up. This will put you more at ease with throwing yourself back into the social whirl. By the time you get to the event you won't feel as anxious. For one, you'll know people who are going to be there. They can introduce you to other people. For another, your friends will be aware that you're anxious. They'll shepherd you. Never be shy about reaching out to people you know for support. As we've learned in the course of this book – that's what friends are for.

Just in case you are you're seeking to move back into having a social life again, after having been a little sequestered, here are some great ways to ease yourself back in:

- Begin by reaching out to acquaintances – the hello-bye bye category is a good place to start. There's not a lot to lose here.

- Extend your social circle to include small groups of people you are friends with, just to observe the dynamics of people relating; familiarizing yourself with being around groups of people again. It doesn't have to be scary. You can ease yourself back in.

- Expand your social circle by accompanying your friends when they are meeting with others. Make it known that you're hoping to move back into a more active social life. Most people will be happy to help you do that.

- Break out of your comfort zone and begin accepting invitations to mix with people, even those not in your close circle of friends. They say that you can't get to the sweetest fruit without going out on a limb, so climb out there. Learn to relish the opportunity to have new experiences with new people. You're learning more about yourself now and about other people. Why not get out there and put some of that knowledge into practice? After all, why shouldn't people want to meet someone as interesting and intelligent as you are?

Be pro-active in socializing

Once you you've become re-acquainted with the practice of seeking out new social connections and when you are no longer in your solitary cocoon, you can begin to pro-actively seek out people you know and others who are new to you. You can begin branching out from the foundation that your friends and acquaintances have provided by moving further into the social milieu, into areas that may be a little unfamiliar. For example:

- Join a group or groups whose members share your hobbies and other interests.

- Enroll to participate in workshops or to pursue courses of study which interest you. It's quite easy to make friends in a group in which all the members share a common interest.

- Volunteer and you'll be happy to serve as you make new friends in the process. While you're at it, you'll develop skills and aptitudes you may have hoped to make more viable. In the same way as workshops or groups, the common core of interest will provide a jumping off point for bonding with others volunteering with you.

- Accept invitations to birthday parties, various celebrations, and other social functions. You never know who'll meet at gathering like these. Break through you own barriers. These may be preventing the type of people you want to connect with from connecting with you.

- Be open to attending social events and even "meet ups", based on common interests. It also doesn't hurt to go out to the bar every now and again. There are people sitting in bars in every city of the world, just looking for someone interesting to talk to. Maybe, just like you, they're looking for a way out of isolation, or social stagnation. Your horizons expand when you demand that they do. No one is going to push them outward for you.

- Join online communities – while these may be located in cyberspace, but I know personally that they can result in real world friendships. I've made many real world friends on Facebook and other online communities. Sometimes, it's easier to share your thoughts in writing, than it is in spoken conversation. This is just one more avenue for making the kind of lasting connections you're hoping to. BONUS: You get to analyze the written communication style of potential new friends before you actually meet them!

Take the initiative

There's no reason you should wait for others to approach you. They're just as reserved as you are, after all. Nobody is born knowing anyone else unless they're family and even then, it's a bit of a crapshoot. You can approach people to start a conversation, by employing simple questions, like "how are you" and "where are you from". It's not hard and you've absolutely nothing to lose. Be open to the people around you and you'll be surprised at how readily they'll respond to that openness.

Remember you are trying to break the ice between you and a stranger, so avoid over-talking. Be warm, but not overly insistent and don't get discouraged if others don't respond immediately. Always try to put yourself in the place of the other person. Employ the lessons you've learned in this book to figure out where they stand and try to meet them there. Be gentle in your judgments of others, though, remembering always that we all judge one another. Take the time to let the person you're engaging revealing themselves to you, just as they're hoping you'll reveal yourself to them.

Fight any temptation to be judgmental

No one's perfect and that includes you. We tend to evaluate people quite harshly before we get to know them. This is a function of our survival instinct, which tells us that the fewer people we allow near us, the less potential there is for danger. But we're modern people and we can do better than that. Besides, you now have in your command a variety of skills concerning non-verbal language that can help you sift through the people who very obviously aren't the sort of folks you're looking for.

Remaining open to those we meet is the door to better friendships and more of them. Not writing people off because of petty complaints about the way they look, or speak, or dress is the best way we can become more flexible about who we welcome as friends and that's the real secret. Sometimes, it's the most unlikely person who is going to prove to be our very best and long-term friend. Everyone is looking for the kind of friends we believe we deserve, but we should always ask ourselves if we meet our own qualifications. You may find that, in asking yourself this question honestly, you discover shortcomings in yourself you might not be willing to tolerate in other people. As I've said repeatedly in this book, knowing yourself is the key to knowing other people, so don't overlook amending your own challenges before you start writing other people off as potential friends, due to their own.

Chapter 7: Manipulation in

a Relationship

In the first book of this series, you were introduced to the basics of influence, mind control, NLP, and manipulation. This book delves deeper, into the subtler manipulation tactics that are often used to influence and sway others. A very important aspect to consider when learning how these tactics work, is **learning how to avoid being a victim or target of a manipulator**.

Many master manipulators have psychopathic tendencies, but not all are in fact true psychopaths, or sociopaths. Some people do not even realize they are trying to exert their will onto another against that person's wishes, but there are those that have the express intent of manipulating others. Psychopaths will actually go out and hunt for people to manipulate, but again, not every manipulative person has a mental defect, nor does every manipulator acknowledge or understand what they are doing.

Being able to determine when someone is attempting to sway you or someone close to you is a fine art. By learning to master the arts of manipulation, influence, mind control, and NLP, you are also mastering the art of spotting these tactics sooner, and saving yourself from undue influence.

The techniques discussed in this book cover an array of relationships, from strangers and new acquaintances, to people that you may already be close to. The most difficult aspect of these tactics to digest is when they are employed against another person in an intimate relationship. The psychological damage that these techniques may cause in a significant other or spouse who has been the victimized or targeted by a manipulative person can last for years. Many people manipulated and used in intimate relationships need to seek out professional psychological effect to help them move past this type of emotional and psychological abuse. And make no mistake, these techniques, when employed against a love one, are abuse.

So, how do you stop yourself from becoming involved with a master manipulator before the relationship develops too far? Well, to begin, it depends if you are engaging in a relationship with someone who just has manipulative tendencies but means you no harm, or a master manipulator who expressly wants to control or manipulate you.

Most intentional manipulators have a few characteristics or traits in common. A lack of empathy is often an ear-mark for a manipulator. They are narcissistic or self-absorbed, and they truly are indifferent to others who suffer for any reason. Their indifference may extend to everyone, but you, and that may make anyone feel special. But special or not, beware, because you will eventually be just another person they feel indifference towards. If you experience a small setback that upsets you, a loss, or an illness, take note of your new partner's actions. Do they state that they care verbally, but refuse to engage with you in person or excuse themselves from you to avoid you during your time of duress? If there is any indication that they may not care as much as they say they do, pay attention for other signs.

While we are on the subject of their words and actions, another easy way to separate the manipulators is not by what they say, but in what they do. Master manipulators are known for being charismatic and saying all the right words at exactly the right times, but rarely do their words and actions match one another. Look for unfulfilled promises, saying one thing and then doing another, and opinions that flipflop, depending on who else is around to hear what they are saying. Manipulators may seem to be all-encompassing to their partners, but in public they may tend to fade into the background in order to observe others, or completely change their stances, opinions, or ideas to fit others they are engaged with. Watch for inconsistencies.

Manipulators who intend to cause harm will tell you they adore you, but find small ways to shoot digs at you that may hurt your feelings. If you are dating or in a relationship with someone who states that they want to spend every waking minute of their free time with you, then calls you "needy" or "codependent" when you express a desire to spend time with you, it is sending mixed signals that you may try to excuse away. There could be a million different reasons why neither of you can spend every day together, but there is never a good excuse to indicate that you are the one with issues, especially when they are the ones who initiated the response from you.

Another consideration to mention again is the right and wrong in a disagreement, and what the manipulator will say and do during an argument. Manipulators will fight dirty, insult you, try and use information you have given them against you, and will never admit wrongdoing. At times, master manipulators will deny words or actions they are aware they have done, hoping that this confusion will make you question your view or beliefs on events that have occurred. They may continue to speak about things that you have expressly stated you no longer want to discuss, creating unease in you, and disregard your discomfort.

Master manipulators will disregard the emotions you express to them. They may refuse to validate the way you feel, or express to you that the way you feel is not accurate or correct. Some manipulative people will begin to completely refuse to acknowledge the feelings of their significant others as the relationship progresses,

Despite all of these negative aspects of the manipulators persona, many people will find that even though they know the relationship is unhealthy, they will continue to engage in the relationship or have an extremely hard time cutting loose from the manipulator. The soaring emotions that excited you in the beginning of the relationship will make you all the more likely to fear losing those strong emotions, and therefore fear losing the manipulator themselves. You may find yourself increasingly unsatisfied in the relationship, and loved ones may notice a change in your mood too, but despite your unhappiness you may find yourself dreading a life without them. Your own mood will begin to be directly controlled by the mood of the manipulator, and you may find yourself attempting to find favor with this person, even though you have done nothing untoward or wrong. Because of the conflicting and confusing aspects of the relationship, you may find yourself overanalyzing or obsessively trying to put your finger on what is really going on. You may notice an increased state or level of anxiety in yourself, as you are unsure of what is happening or where you stand with the manipulative partner. Apologizing or compromising who you are regularly, whether you understand why you feel the need, feeling insecure about yourself in general, or experiencing feelings of guilt or inadequacy are often strong indicators that you are in a relationship with a manipulator.

The best way to protect yourself from engaging in a manipulative relationship is to be aware of their often-subtle manipulation tactics. The next chapter will begin to educate you in the often-used subtle arts of master manipulators, and will include examples of these techniques. Again, it should go without saying that these nuanced tactics can be used by you, or against you, in any interaction, and at any level of familiarity.

the Workplace

The workplace is a fertile ground for manipulation of various types to occur. Many people will find they encounter at least several of the following types of workplace manipulators over the course of their career. It can be hard to know how to draw the line between normal workplace politics, gossip and banter and actual manipulation. By being able to identify some of the main types of manipulators that exist within the world of work it can help potential targets to stay away from the wrong type of colleague before they find their world has been turned upside down and their professional life damaged beyond repair.

The Blackmailer

The Blackmailer is a type of workplace manipulator that can have a serious impact not only on their victims' careers but also on their mental wellbeing and overall sanity. The basic method of the blackmailer is to appear friendly and highly trustworthy at first. This is usually achieved by finding a newcomer to the workplace or someone who does not fit in with others particularly well.

Once a suitable target has been identified the blackmailer will invest a serious amount of time and effort in winning over their target and deceptively earning their trust. This is often done by taking a new member of staff under their wing and offering to mentor them and make their new life at the company as easy as possible.

The blackmailer will often form a friendship with their intended target that occurs outside of work as well as inside work. This is essential as for the blackmailer's manipulation to be effective it must involve the target seeing the blackmailer more as a trusted friend than simply as a colleague.

Over time, the blackmailer will begin to subtly elicit sensitive information from their target. This could involve controversial opinions about the other people that the two work with or even sensitive details of the victim's personal life such as their sexual orientation or political views. The blackmailer will keep going until they feel they have accumulated a sufficient amount of information to use against their victim.

Once the blackmailer has some powerful information to hold against their target, such as a covert phone recording of them saying something disparaging, or a photograph of the target behaving controversially in some way, the blackmailer will begin to hold it against them. They may make threats such as planning to reveal the sensitive information to others within the workplace or even the target's loved ones and family.

The blackmailer will often demand increasing levels of money or favors from the victim in order to keep their secrets safe. The victim ends up living in a constant state of fear as they do not know when and if they will have their secrets revealed. This has a destructive effect on the victim's mental health and can lead to breakdowns and major levels of anxiety.

The False Ally

The false ally is a type of workplace manipulator who is skilled at hiding their true intentions. They will seem to be a keen ally of their target. They are likely to suggest to their target that together they will go big places in the workplace and support each other's climb up the career ladder.

The false ally will often begin by making an over the top show of helping out their intended target. This is designed to ensure that the target sees them as a trustworthy figure and also feels a debt of gratitude towards the false ally. Once the false ally feels they have earned the trust and respect of their target they will begin to exert subtle levels of control over them.

Some typical plays in the playbook of the false ally include coercing a victim into acting in the self-interest of the ally and not of the victim. This will usually take place under the guise of doing 'what's best for both of us' when in actual fact it will be anything but. This type of manipulation is especially effective if the victim is naive and idealistic. The false ally is able to tap into the desires and ambitions of the victim in order to gain their compliance in carrying out the false ally's bidding.

The endgame of the false ally is typically to see their own career advance while their target's either stalls or is damaged irreparably.

This often takes the form of the false ally gaining some form of recognition, like a promotion, at the expense of the target, but due to the efforts and choices the target has been coerced into. Often, the victim has no idea that they have been played like a puppet until it is too late and the false ally has already benefited.

The Abuser of Power

It is a well known fact that power has the potential to corrupt human beings. The workplace is one of the most common arenas for such behavior to occur. The abuse of power can take many different forms but they all involve someone unfairly wielding a position of hierarchical authority over another person.

Some common examples of abuses of power include those in supervisory or management positions asking for inappropriate or over the top levels of support and compliance from those they have power over. This can take less serious forms, such as getting workers to put in hours that they are not paid for or take more serious forms such as pressuring female employees into sexual liaisons in exchange for the promise of promotions and job security.

It is important to draw a distinction between someone who exerts power in a legitimate fashion and someone who abuses it. In order for the wielding of power to cross the line into the realms of covert emotional manipulation it must fulfill the following criteria. Firstly, the manipulator must have a position of authority over their target, such as by being their manager or some other formal position of authority. Secondly, the manipulator must use their power in a way which is intended to control their victim through the manipulation of their emotions. Abusers of power can draw on aspects such as their victim's feelings of job insecurity or doubt about their future.

Abusers of power are particularly dangerous types of manipulators as they have very little chance of being caught. This is due to the fact that it can be difficult for someone within a workplace to blame their boss or superior for their own actions. Unless clear evidence exists, which it very rarely does, then it is likely to come down to the word of the victim against the word of the manipulator. Sadly, this is rarely sufficient evidence for a company to take any kind of action against the person who has abused the power they hold.

The Sexual Predator

Sexual predators can take the form of almost any other type of workplace manipulator but also exist on their own. Simply put, a sexual predator is one who seeks to act in an inappropriate sexual way towards someone they work with. This can range in severity.

At one end of the scale, workplace sexual predators may simply make another member of staff feel uncomfortable. This can be through looks, gestures or inappropriate physical contact. Despite this being the most mild type of sexual predatory behavior that can occur, it is still incredibly serious and should be avoided at all costs.

Sadly, many workplace sexual predators take things a lot further than merely making a victim feel uncomfortable. Many sexual predators will coerce their victim into carrying out behaviors of a sexual nature that they feel pressured or forced into doing. In order to ensure that their victim stays quiet about what has occurred, the predator will often gather some kind of compromising evidence, such as photographs, which the predator threatens to expose to the victim's colleagues and family should they cause any problems for the predator.

Although many workplaces have policies in place which are intended to protect against any type of inappropriate sexual behavior in the workplace they are rarely enough to stop the worst predators from going about their manipulation. This is due to the fact that skilled predators of this nature are able to ensure they do not leave any evidence whatsoever. They are also likely to choose victims who have low self-esteem or have some other reason that makes them unlikely to tell others of what has taken place.

The Bully

Bullies may seem to be a fairly trivial type of workplace manipulator but this is far from the case. Bullying can have a severe impact upon someone's happiness and wellbeing and is often hard to detect and even harder to stop. This is due to the fact that a skilled manipulator engaged in the practice of bullying is likely to mask their actions as friendship or advice. Underneath the friendly veneer, however, something far more dangerous and sinister is occurring.

Bullying can range in severity. On one end of the scale, a bully may seem to be making jokes that just happen to involve the victim. However, this is not what is happening. What seems like a joke is often actually an attempt to gradually erode the victim's confidence and leave them vulnerable and doubtful. A cognitive dissonance is created in the victim's mind as on the one hand they are aware that the comments or actions of the bully are hurting them but on the other they do not want to appear overly sensitive or thin skinned. This often results in the victim begrudgingly accepting the bullying that is taking place, even if it is hurting them in the long run.

In order for bullying to work the manipulator chooses their target carefully. They are likely to select someone who lacks self-confidence and is not particularly popular within the workplace. This is due to the fact that the victim will put up with the bullying as it is often the only form of attention they have received in the workplace up until that point.

Bullying can have severe consequences in the long run. It can chip away at the victim's confidence and happiness and, perversely, create a sense of dependency on the manipulator and the attention they provide. The effects can be with a victim for the rest of their life. They may have severe difficulty in trusting another again and forming any type of healthy relationship in the future. This is due to the fact they will have fallen into the pattern of seeking approval and validation via negative attention.

Chapter 8: Tips and Tricks to Defend Yourself from Manipulation

Now that we have gone over some of the methods and tactics people use to negatively manipulate others, it's time to talk about how to avoid these methods. Negative manipulation can be defined as convincing others to do whatever you desire, without offering something of value back to them. How does this phenomenon work?

- **A Threat and no Value:** If a person says, "Help me finish this project or I'm going to be angry with you," they are trying to negatively manipulate your actions. They are not actually offering anything of value to you in return. However, if a friend offers you something of value in return for a favor, that isn't negative manipulation, because you're getting something back for the effort you put in.

- **Making another Responsible for their Emotions:** Another form of manipulation is telling someone that they are responsible for how you feel and that they should feel guilty for that. For example, telling them that if they don't come to your party, you will be highly disappointed. This implies that it's their fault how you feel. However, if you offer to introduce your friend to someone they have been wanting to meet at your party, you are offering a situation that allows both of you to win.

Why do People Manipulate?

What are people's reasons for manipulating others? These can be anything from innocent and even friendly reasons to mean and selfish, but for the sake of this chapter, we're going to focus on negative and selfish manipulation.

- **Misery Likes Company:** They do it because they gain satisfaction, on an emotional level, from seeing the frustrated or otherwise negative responses of others. Certain people are so unhappy with their lives and themselves that they try to bring others down by creating problems for them.

- **It makes them feel Powerful:** Someone who is insecure and feels powerless will often try to exert power in other areas to make up for it. Getting others to do what they want gives them temporary satisfaction.

- **A Lack of Importance:** Another reason why people negatively manipulate others is because they don't think that they are important. They believe that if they simply request what they wish for, they won't get it because they don't matter enough. So instead, they try to make us feel ashamed or guilty as a consequence for not doing what they want, as a preemptive measure from disappointment.

- **They are "too Good" for some Things:** Other negative manipulators simply think that they are too good for certain tasks. They might see other people as below them, and therefore expect those people to do the tasks that they don't want to do. This could be due to laziness, or simply an inflated sense of self.

- **Not Knowing how to get Things done:** Some negative manipulators don't think that they are capable of gaining what they want, and instead operate under the assumption that they must convince and pressure others to do their bidding for them.

- **Selfishly "Helping" Others:** Other negative manipulators actually convince themselves that what they are doing will help people. This is a common idea embraced by people who think that they know better than others what is best for everyone. Due to their beliefs that they have a higher intelligence or ability, they feel satisfied doing this, and convince themselves that the people being manipulated are better off for it.

Actually, the majority of negative manipulators are not actually bad people; they are simply misguided, inconsiderate, insensitive, selfish, and often times, weak and insecure. Some of them believe that the people they are manipulating are not as valuable as themselves, and that their desires and needs are not as important. This mistaken belief is what allows them to continue to act the way they do without considering the feelings of other people.

Different types of Negative Manipulation:

- **Turning your Emotions against you:** Techniques for manipulation vary widely, but usually, negative manipulators will attempt to get the feelings of others to work against them. They will try to do that by doing or saying things that are intended to stir up fear, anger, shame, guilt, or any other uncomfortable feeling. For example, they might insinuate that if we don't follow through on their suggestions or orders, something horrible will result.

- **Threats of Future Unpleasantness:** They might also try to describe to you all of the different types of unpleasant situations that could arise if you don't do what they want. They might imply or even overtly insist that something is our fault, responsibility, or duty, using ethics and morality to pressure us to come around to their ideas or demands. Some people will even throw every trick at us, warning us of the consequences of disappointing or letting them down.

- **Common Phrases Used:** They may imply to us that we will be so happy if we do what they want us to do, or that we will make them very happy, and that they will love us so much. They may also use phrases like "You need to..." or "You must..." or "You should..." as a way to subtly pressure you into following through on what they are asking of you. They will say those phrases and others which insinuate great consequences if you don't follow the obligation they are giving to you.

What do each of the above methods and techniques share in common with each other? The person doing the negative manipulation doesn't offer anything of value in return for fulfilling their wishes. Instead, the victim gets exploited by a created power imbalance.

How to Avoid being Negatively Manipulated by Others:

So, now that we have discussed some of the signs of negative manipulation, it's time to figure out how to avoid it and recognize when someone is trying to use it on you.

- **Be Aware of your Rights:** The absolute most important rule you can follow when dealing with someone who wants to manipulate you in negative ways is to know your own worth and rights. This way, you will always know when someone is attempting to violate them. So long as others are not getting harmed in the process, you should be defending yourself. Every human should have the right to have differing opinions from others, to protect yourself, to say "no" when you need to, and to decide what's important to you. You should also have the right of expressing your wants, opinions, and feelings, and always be treated with respect.

- Unfortunately, the world has plenty of people who won't want to acknowledge or respect your rights, especially negative manipulators. You will also come into contact with others who generally wish to take advantage at any opportunity. However, you can proudly defy this by letting them know that you are the one who runs your life, no one else.

- **Maintain Healthy Distance:** Another way to tell who is manipulative is to pay attention to the way someone acts in varying situations and in front of various individuals. Although everyone, to a degree, puts on different faces depending on where they are, most people who are harmfully manipulative are extreme about it. They might, for example, be extremely polite and friendly to one person, and completely disrespect another, or act like a victim one second, and then act controlling immediately after.

- If you notice someone acting this way regularly, it's a good sign to distance yourself from them and not engage with them unless it's an absolute necessity. Usually, the reasons behind these types of behavior are complicated, and it isn't your duty or responsibility to help or change that person. Trying to do so will often only lead to suffering on your part, so it's better not to expect much when you notice these signs.

- **Don't Blame yourself:** A person who wishes to manipulate others in harmful ways searches for weaknesses to exploit, so it makes sense that someone who has been victimized by one might blame themselves or feel inadequate. But in a situation like this, you should remember that it isn't you that's the issue here; you are being pressured to feel bad by someone else who is very good at making people feel bad.

- This is how they get their way. Instead, think about the relationship you have with this person and ask yourself if they are respecting you, demanding reasonable things of you, and whether you are both benefiting, or only one of you is. Ask yourself, also, if you feel good about yourself after spending time with this person, or if you would feel better being around them less. The way you answer these questions will lead to important answers about where the issue lies in the situation.

- **Questioning them:** Eventually, this type of person is going to demand or request things from you. Many times, these requests or others will take their needs into consideration, while completely ignoring yours. Next time you receive a solicitation that is completely unreasonable, turn the focus back to them by asking some questions. Ask them if their request is reasonable, or if what they are asking from you is fair. You can also try asking if you get to have an opinion in this matter, or ask what benefit you will be gaining from the arrangement.

- Each time you ask questions like this, you are holding a mirror up to them, allowing them to see what they are truly asking of you. If they are self-aware, they will likely retract their request or demand. But there may be some cases, such as dealing with a narcissist, who will keep insisting without even considering your questions. If that happens, follow these guidelines.

- **Don't Answer Immediately:** One way to combat manipulation is to use time as a resource. Often, the manipulator will not only ask you to fulfill an unreasonable demand, but they will want an answer immediately. When this happens, rather than answering right away, use time and distance yourself from their request and influence. This can be done by telling them that you will think about it. Although these words are simple, they give your power back to you, giving you the option to weigh the advantages and disadvantages of the situation and let you work out something better, if need be.

- **Teach yourself to say "No" when needed:** Saying "no" is difficult for many people, since we are often taught and conditioned to be polite whenever possible. Being able to confidently but politely say "no" comes with learning communication skills. When this is articulated effectively, you can hold onto your self-respect, and also continue a healthy relationship. Keep in mind that your personal rights include deciding what matters to you, being able to turn down a request free from guilt, and choosing health and happiness for yourself. You are responsible for your life, not the person who is making unreasonable demands of you.

- **Create a Consequence:** Next time a negative manipulator tries to violate your rights, and refuses to accept your answer, set a consequence for their behavior. Knowing how to assert and identify appropriate consequences is a crucial skill for standing down someone who is being very difficult or disrespectful. If you can articulate this clearly and thoroughly, your consequences will cause them to pause and stop violating you, shifting to a position of respect.

How to Confront a Bully in a Safe Way:

Not all manipulators resort to bullying, but many of them do. Someone is being a bully when they use intimidation or harm to get what they want from you. Remember, always, that a bully chooses people they see as weak to pick on, and compliance and passivity will only strengthen this. However, a lot of bullies are afraid and insecure deep down, so when their victim starts to stand up for themselves, this will often lead the bully to back off. Whether this situation is occurring in a playground or at the office, it applies, most of the time. Keep in mind that many bullies have actually withstood bullying and violence. Although this doesn't excuse their behaviors, it does help the victim to understand.

Your Influence Skill Set

<u>Clarity of purpose</u>

An important facet of the ability to influence others is your own clarity. Know what you want and have a clear plan of how you're going to get it. Whether you're working in sales and trying to improve the team's quarterly figures, or trying to encourage a student to be more diligent with study, or to set them on a career path – know what the objective is, clearly. The only way you can succeed in influencing someone to behave in a desired way, is if you are clear about what you hope to achieve. You don't get in your car to drive to a destination you've never been without setting the GPS. The same goes for the application of influence toward achieving a desired effect or goal. Know where you're going.

Always be prepared in advance, with the following:

- A list of prioritized objectives.

- A clear picture of the final destination (what it looks like).

Preparing the environment

If you are seeking to reach agreement with someone, you need to make them feel comfortable. You also need to be relaxed, yourself. At the same time, for effective communication (which is important when you want to influence someone's behavior, as this book is explaining) you need to make the environment conducive to your interaction. And you need to have in place a planned sequence of events at that meeting beforehand.

The best way to achieve this is to draw up a meeting agenda and circulate it to those who will attend, one day prior to the meeting. In this way, everyone knows what to expect and what shape the meeting will take. The agenda should make clear what the goals of the meeting are. Checking off the items on it should move you closer to agreement, if not enable all present to reach consensus to move forward. The logical sequence of events represented by following an agenda is a function of a critically structured plan. Having a plan of such quality never fails to impress.

Consensus building

In building consensus, you're making it clear you are open to suggestion (which you should always be, regardless of your single minded focus on your ultimate goal). Building consensus employs those listening skills we talked about earlier. Hearing what people say and truly listening means you're not planning a response while they're talking. It means you're actively hearing everything they say. Subtext, word choice and tone are all important and so are your skills at hearing what's really being said. Proceeding with these skills in play can provide you with the basis for genuine and not false consensus.

False consensus is reached when people are "heard out", but not "heard". These are two entirely different animals. The first is condescending indulgence of hearing what no longer matters, because a decision has already been made and the results of that decision, imposed. Being heard means that influence on the final decision is still a possibility and that what's offered may result in concessions, if it features actual merit.

Being present to the input of others and being able to integrate their thoughts and suggestions into an existing plan is a function of leadership. Leadership is not imposed. Leadership is extended to others as a service. Consensus building is a way to bring forward the knowledge of the team and add it to your own. In the case of reaching agreement, it's the foundation of lasting relationships that won't later be ruptured by objections to not being heard. This is extremely important. Autocratic leadership is unwelcome and will not survive for long. It is a corrosive leadership style that is not sustainable.

Creating rapport

When someone begins to enjoy your company, it becomes much easier for you to enlist their support. This makes it more likely they'll support your viewpoint in situations in which that counts. Allies are people who like and trust you. Your relationships are what will move your goals forward and create a foundation for your success and that of your allies, also. People, while perhaps not being entirely aware of this on an intellectual level, know this instinctively. That is why it is important that you prioritize establishing rapport with others. It's the basis of strong allegiances.

Part of creating rapport is establishing the common interests you hold with others. Taking an interest in them and offering them information about who you are is how this is achieved. Being too veiled about yourself makes you appear cold, calculating and detached. Establish that you're open and also, a person who can be trusted.

It's also important to establish ease with others and one way this can done is to mirror body language. You'll probably find (if you pay attention), that you do this anyway, when you've begun to establish rapport with someone. Mirroring body language sends the unconscious signal that there is a bond already established between two people and that they're on the same team. Mirroring speech patterns is another way of doing this. Repeating key words with enthusiasm at opportune times is another natural way we tell each other we're enjoying a conversation or agreeing with each other. Nod, smile and respond positively when you sense a common theme emerging in conversation. This sends the message that you're accessible on the most basic, human level.

Suggestions instead of demands

People routinely bridle at directives. In Western societies where individualism is a way of life, we like to believe in our personal autonomy as a value. That means it's not the best course of action to demand things from people. Much more effective is suggesting a course of action and building consensus based on the suggestion, while being open to input and concessions to other points of view. This is the democratic way of achieving goals and one that is completely manageable with the application of a deft hand.

Here are examples of language that gives your listener the option to chip in and yet still leaves you the "wiggle room" to get to where you believe you need to go:

- Would you be interested in doing a-b-c?

- Could you be interested in doing a-b-c?

- I think we should do a-b-c. What do you think?

- Do you think this is the best way forward, or do you have others ideas?

Leaving space for opinion and input, while still advancing the validity of your own opinion is the stuff of which influence is made. While you're providing people with a rationale for your point of view, your willingness to entertain amendments to that point of view only increases your influential power. Imposition rarely ends in anything but resentment. By building consensus through input and exchange, you will still arrive at the goal you have in mind, but you'll do it with the support of a willing team, signed on to the plan in question. A fringe benefit? That input will undoubtedly improve on the original plan and will result in satisfaction on the part of all involved.

Heightening your awareness

Awareness of the responses of other people to what you're saying is a key to influential action. What are their facial expressions telling you? Their body language and their word choices? What about tone and pitch? All these factors are rich with information that you can draw on to temper your pitch and to get people on your side. It can also cue you to back off and change lanes, while you re-group and allow others their input.

Active listening, while employing body language (head nodding, eye contact) and assenting noises ("uh-huh", "yes", "I see") is also about deeply engaging with what's being said and the complementary messages being sent by the speaker. Your awareness in crucial situations, of all the factors that create a communicative environment, is of the utmost important. You need to be aware, not only of what's being said, but implications about what's intended, what's not being said and the speaker's frame of mind. All these factors work together to form a more concise body of information from which you may draw in order to apply influential action.

Conclusion

While outright mimicry is obviously out of the question, you can certainly seek to mirror the communication styles of the people you're engaging with, in order to help you establish rapport and common ground. Suppose someone looks at you for just a couple of seconds before looking down, or past you, and then looks back at you. This non-verbal style tells you something important about the person you're engaging – sustained eye contact is undesirable. So mirror that, in order to establish a comfortable level of communication that's implicitly agreed upon by both parties. This is an unspoken level of communication. By mirroring the tendencies of the other party, you are sending a message of respect and concession to the communication style being modelled.

At the conclusion of a business interaction, especially a meeting, it's important that you provide a summation of what you came into that meeting intending to do. In the course of your summation, you can acknowledge the importance of the feedback and input the exchange or meeting has provided. Pointing out that the feedback received was pivotal to the development of your agenda and enriched it, gets people on your bus and ready to roll. When people feel their opinions are valued, they will come along for the ride. They will also form part of a team that is more cohesive than if you hadn't included and then acknowledged the role their input played in reinforcing your foundational agenda.

The addition of the input of others to your narrative is a key component of consensus building as a part of influential action. It's a form of leadership outreach that not only strengthens the leader's position, but strengthens the agenda's integrity. Adding useful feedback and input can only build a better mousetrap. Good and successful leaders are keenly aware of this.